GUIDE TO RIGHTS CLEARANCE & PERMISSIONS

IN SCHOLARLY, EDUCATIONAL AND TRADE PUBLISHING

STEPHEN E. GILLEN

Guide to Rights Clearance and Permissions in Scholarly, Educational, and Trade Publishing

By Stephen E. Gillen

Copyright © 2018 by Stephen E. Gillen
All rights reserved. No part of this book may be used, transmitted, or reproduced in any form or by any means, electronic or mechanical, including photocopying and recording, or by any information storage and retrieval system, without the prior written permission of the publisher, except for brief quotations in reviews of the work.

We encourage you to quote brief passages from this work for use in reviews or for scholarly or critical works. For longer passages, reprints, or other uses, you will need to obtain our written permission and we ask that you direct your request to:

Textbook & Academic Authors Association (TAA)
PO Box 367, Fountain City, WI 54629. Phone: (727) 563-0020. Email: Info@TAAonline.net

This publication is designed to provide accurate and authoritative information with regard to the subject matter covered. It is sold with the understanding that the publisher is not engaged in rendering legal, accounting, or other professional advice. If legal advice or other expert assistance is required, the services of a competent professional person should be sought. —From a *Declaration of Principles* jointly adopted by a Committee of the American Bar Association and a Committee of Publishers and Associations

Publication Manager and Editor: Kim Pawlak, Director of Publishing & Operations, TAA
Indexer: J. Naomi Linzer Indexing Services
Cover & Interior Design: Jim Shubin, BookAlchemist.net

ISBN: 978-0-9975004-3-1
Library of Congress Control Number: 201893165

Publisher's Cataloging-In-Publication Data
(Prepared by The Donohue Group, Inc.)

Names: Gillen, Stephen E., 1953-

Title: Guide to rights clearance & permissions in scholarly, educational, and trade publishing / Stephen E. Gillen.

Other Titles: Guide to rights clearance and permissions in scholarly, educational, and trade publishing

Description: Fountain City, WI : Textbook & Academic Authors Association (TAA), [2018] | Includes index.

Identifiers: ISBN 9780997500431 | ISBN 9780997500448 (ebook)

Subjects: LCSH: Copyright licenses--United States--Handbooks, manuals, etc. | Fair use (Copyright)--United States--Handbooks, manuals, etc. | Press law Handbooks, manuals, etc. | Open access publishing--Law and legislation--Handbooks, manuals, etc.

Classification: LCC KF3020 .G55 2018 (print) | LCC KF3020 (ebook) | DDC 346.7304/82--dc23

The Textbook & Academic Authors Association (TAA) provides a wide range of professional development resources, events and networking opportunities for textbook authors and authors of scholarly journal articles and books. Visit www.TAAonline.net.

WHAT READERS ARE SAYING ABOUT
Guide to Rights Clearance & Permissions in Scholarly, Educational, and Trade Publishing:

"*Guide to Rights Clearance & Permissions* contains essential information that will help authors steer safely through the sometimes treacherous waters of copyrights, fair use, permissions, and scholarly integrity. Mr. Gillen makes legal issues easy to understand, interesting, and at times downright fascinating. Even experienced authors who think they've 'seen it all' are likely to be surprised by some of the information that can be gleaned from this book." —June Jamrich Parsons, author of *New Perspectives on Computer Concepts*

"In Gillen's usual style, he covers topics that are well beyond the expertise of most authors in a way that makes important principles easy to understand and implement. I have already used this handy guide to find clear and useful answers to some of my questions about trademarking book titles and finding copyright holders." —Kevin Patton, PhD, author of *Anatomy & Physiology, 10e*

"In today's litigious environment, Steve Gillen's *Guide to Rights Clearance & Permissions* is a godsend to all authors who want to avoid being sued. This invaluable guide also presents a set of priceless templates that will save authors incredible time and anguish in obtaining and tracking permissions." —Dr. Mary Ellen Guffey, Cengage author of three market-leading college textbooks

"In this new book, Gillen tackles the complexities of clearing intellectual property rights in an expert, comprehensive, and highly readable fashion, and advises how to avoid legal jeopardy from the misuse of copyrighted materials. My reaction is the same as after reading Gillen's other invaluable publications: I wish I knew all this then!" —Fred S. Kleiner, Professor of History of Art & Architecture, Professor of Archaeology, Boston University, textbook author

"Steve Gillen's book is a concise and straightforward explanation of the issues that arise from the rights clearance process. It's thorough, well-written, and accessible to non-lawyers; it's a valuable resource for anyone who needs to understand the rights and permissions process." —Ashley Messenger, Senior Associate General Counsel, National Public Radio, and author of *A Practical Guide to Media Law*

"Stephen Gillen's *Guide to Rights Clearance & Permissions* is an invaluable 'how-to' for identifying and avoiding the legal pitfalls surrounding issues of fair use, infringement, privacy, and plagiarism that can accompany publishing—and that's just the short list of what you'll find inside. Whether you are an author wishing to minimize your liability in publishing a work, or a publishing professional with a permissions and licensing program of your own, you'll find a wealth of good, practical advice in this book."
—Barbara Price, PhD, textbook editor/publishing professional

"For more than two decades, Stephen's teachings led me to take care with permissions and clearances in my own texts and to be attentive to others as they utilized elements of my work in their books. His lessons were and are invaluable to me. Now, with this new book, Stephen brings all this wisdom and knowledge to us in a concise, well-written guide." —Robert Christopherson, author of *Geosystems, 9e*

"*Guide to Rights Clearance and Permissions* is a comprehensive, easy-to-understand explanation of one of the most challenging and vexing responsibilities faced by textbook writers. This practical guide is an invaluable resource to understanding the evolving and increasingly stringent applications of copyright laws to the use of third-party content. Authors will want to keep this book handy—and consult it again and again when writing or revising a manuscript." —Sean W. Wakely, Vice President, Product and Editorial, FlatWorld

"In this book, Steve lends his considerable experience and expertise to bear on the myriad of issues surrounding the intricacies of the rights and permissions process for intellectual property holders and users everywhere. A valuable reference for all of those who spend our time dealing with these issues on an ongoing, and even occasional, basis." —Chris Will, Publishing and Education Professional

TABLE OF CONTENTS

(9) INTRODUCTION

(12) CHAPTER 1. COPYRIGHT PRIMER
First Things First: Parsing Copyright Protection........... 13
Examining Exceptions.. 16
Creative Commons and Open Educational Resources...18
Self-Published Works and Use of Your Own Work........19
University Licenses..20
Caution for Those Writing Scholarly Works..................20

(23) CHAPTER 2. THE FAIR USE DEFENSE
More Fair Use Cases..26
Practical Pointers and Guidelines.................................27
Caution for Those Writing Scholarly Works..................28

(29) CHAPTER 3. AVOIDING THE NEED FOR PERMISSIONS
The Potential Claims...31
Practical Pointers and Guidelines.................................34
Attribution, Authorship, and Scholarly Integrity........... 36

(40) CHAPTER 4. DEFAMATION PRIMER
What Do the Numbers Tell Us?.................................... 40
What Are the Elements of a Libel Claim?..................... 41
Libel Tourism Hazards...45
The Right-to-Be-Forgotten Risks................................. 47
Fiction/Faction Dangers..48
Protection Possibilities..51
Practical Guidelines..52

(55) CHAPTER 5. PRIVACY PRIMER
Publication of Private Facts.. 56
Intrusion into Seclusion...57
False Light..57
Practical Pointers and Guidelines.................................58

CHAPTER 6. RIGHT OF PUBLICITY — 60
Practical Pointers and Guidelines 62

CHAPTER 7. SPECIAL CONSIDERATIONS FOR ENDORSEMENTS AND TESTIMONIALS — 64
Reader Endorsements 65
Expert Endorsements 66
Bloggers 66
Reviewers 67
Disclosures and Disclaimers 67
Different Rules for the Inside and Outside 68

CHAPTER 8. TRADEMARK PRIMER — 70
Limitations on Use of Third-Party Marks 72
Using Trademarks Proactively 73
Registration 77
The Upside 80
Copyrights Distinguished 81
Single Works vs. Series 82
Why Go to the Trouble and Expense? 84
The Downside 85

CHAPTER 9. WHAT YOU NEED TO KNOW ABOUT USING THIRD-PARTY PHOTOS — 87
Categories of Use: Editorial vs. Commercial 89
Categories of Assets: Royalty-Free vs.
   Rights-Managed vs. Commissioned Work 90
Limitations on Use 91
Consequences 94

CHAPTER 10. SPECIAL CONSIDERATIONS FOR MUSIC — 96
Use of Song Lyrics in Text 96
Other Uses of Music 97
Practical Pointers and Guidelines 102

CHAPTER 11. SPECIAL CONSIDERATIONS FOR ART — 104

CHAPTER 12. FINDING THE COPYRIGHT OWNER — 107
The Problem of Orphan Works..................................108
Practical Solutions: Building a Record of Diligence.....110

CHAPTER 13. CONTRACTS AND THE ALLOCATION OF RESPONSIBILITY FOR PERMISSIONS MATTERS — 115
Your Representations and Warranties.........................117
The Teeth: Indemnification and Defense Obligations...123

CHAPTER 14. DEPICTION RELEASES, PROPERTY RELEASES, LOCATION RELEASES, AND PERMITS — 126
Depiction Releases...127
Property and Location Releases..................................128
Permits...130

CHAPTER 15. INSURANCE AND RESERVES FOR MANAGING RISK — 131
Types of Insurance..131
The Application Process..132
Claims-Made vs. Occurrence-Based Policies.................133
Cost..134
Acceptable Business Risk and Reserving for
   After-the-Fact Permissions......................................134

CHAPTER 16. PERMISSIONS, RECORD KEEPING, AND DUE DILIGENCE — 136
Obtaining Permissions..137
Record Keeping..139
Minors..140
Abiding by Contract Terms...141
Permissions the Other Way..142
Good Reasons to Improve Your Permissions
   Program...143
Permissions Best Practices..145
How Do You Price the Grant?....................................146

8 GUIDE TO RIGHTS CLEARANCE & PERMISSIONS

(148) CHAPTER 17. DEALING WITH THE CEASE AND DESIST LETTER
What Do You Do Next??..148
Going It Alone..149
The Question Worth Asking..151
Don't Rise to the Bait..152
Ignore Most of the Demands, Most of the Time,
  at Least Initially...152
Be Careful Out There...153

(158) RESOURCES

(161) TEMPLATES
Request for Permission to Reprint Text......................162
Request for Permission to Reprint Text
  (Alternate Form)..163
Request for Permission to Reprint Photograph...........164
Photo Release, No Fee...165
Photo Release, Fee..166
Video Release, Uncompensated..................................167
Professional Model Release.......................................168
Release for Use of Physical Location..........................171
Personal Property Release...173
Photography/Videography Permit Application............175
Interview Release..177
Depiction and Collaboration Agreement.....................179
Permissions Log..184

(185) GLOSSARY

(194) INDEX

INTRODUCTION

IN THE UNITED STATES, THE FIRST AMENDMENT PROVIDES us, as authors and publishers, with great freedom in the formulation and presentation of our message. Nonetheless, there are meaningful constraints on what we can say and how we can say it, including the following:

- the law of defamation obliges us to be careful with the facts
- the law of privacy limits our ability to seek and disclose highly personal information without the subject's consent
- the right of publicity restrains us from unauthorized exploitation of a person's name, likeness, or persona to sell an unrelated product or service
- copyright law places limits on what we can copy or adapt from pre-existing works
- trademark law precludes us from using the brands of another in a way that confuses the public about source, affiliation, or endorsement
- contract law holds us to the promises we sometimes make in the course of obtaining access to information or content

What follows is some background information about these areas of law together with information and advice for avoiding or managing the risk of a claim against you or securing permission if avoidance is unworkable.

Although this discussion focuses principally on U.S. law, similar concerns may arise under the laws of other nations. These issues can arise any time a publication crosses national boundaries, whether in a traditional format, such as a printed magazine, or in a newer medium, such as electronic publication or content made available via social media or a website.

In the chapters that follow, we'll turn our attention first to copyright matters, the central issue that will drive the majority of rights clearance and permissions needs you will confront. We'll look at copyright basics. We'll examine fair use, the principal exception to the monopoly rights vested in copyright owners. And we'll look at techniques for circumventing the need to get copyright permissions.

We'll turn next to defamation and privacy matters, the right of publicity, and trademarks. Not every potential publication risk can be addressed by securing permission. Some risks arise simply from what you say or disclose about your subject. A business case may include information or descriptions that are unflattering or even offensive to the executive or business being profiled. Sometimes this risk can be abated with a depiction release. More often, you just have to be careful about what you write.

In Chapters 1 through 3 we pay special attention to the unique issues that confront those writing scholarly and scientific works—considerations like attributing text and ideas borrowed from others; fair use; dealing with authorship credit; variations in rights-clearing strategies from field to field; the upside-down business model of open access journal writing; the non-exclusive rights reserved by some universities to the writings of their faculty; whether self-publishing affects the potential to publish traditionally in the future; and the variability in licensing models for open educational resources.

We'll take a closer look at special cases—photographs, music, and art—where it is useful to understand the unique business models and licensing norms (and even specialized terminology) that have evolved over time.

But even before we get to the long list of possible claims and how they might be addressed, you may want to consider whose job this is (or ought to be)—should the author take the lead? Should the publisher do it? Or should it be a shared obligation? Regardless of which role you're in, if you are about to sign a publishing contract, read Chapter 13 first.

We'll look at strategies for dealing with risk, including the use of releases and permission requests, as well as insurance and reserves. We'll address a strategy for requesting permission, when you should do this, how best to go about it, what to do if you don't get it, and how to respond if you get a letter from someone complaining.

We'll provide you with a list of resources for more in-depth information on the topics we present here. And finally, we'll equip you with some templates for commonly used forms, letters, and agreements to get you started.

1) COPYRIGHT PRIMER

THE PROBLEMS YOU WILL MOST COMMONLY CONFRONT in clearing the rights necessary to publish your book, journal article, or multi-media work will be copyright problems. What is covered by copyright? Who owns those rights. How long do they last? Are there ever exceptions? All of these questions are addressed in the pages that follow. Pay close attention. No area of law is as widely misunderstood by folks who ought to know better than is copyright law.

> ### "BUT HONESTLY, MONICA..."
>
> With these three words, the publisher of *Cooks Source* magazine launched an impatient email response to a writer's infringement complaint.
>
> Then she continued: "... the web is considered 'public domain' and you should be happy we just didn't 'lift' your whole article and put someone else's name on it!"
>
> Unfortunately for her magazine, she couldn't have been more wrong about the copyright implications of Web posting. And although her misconception is all too

> commonly shared, her error—compounded no doubt by her condescending tone—ignited an Internet firestorm. The email went instantly viral; the publisher's email and voicemail accounts were stuffed overnight with scathing messages; the magazine's Facebook page was assaulted by "fans" posting mocking comments; Twitter buzzed with 140-character taunts tagged #buthonestlymonica; satirical videos popped up on YouTube; and advertisers fled, forcing the magazine to close within weeks.
>
> Every copyright mistake is not so instantly and irrevocably fatal, but a persistent supply of copyright mistakes and misconceptions seems to be working mischief in two directions—in some cases causing publishers and writers to take what they should be asking for; and in other cases, causing them to shy away from uses that are probably fair.

FIRST THINGS FIRST: PARSING COPYRIGHT PROTECTION

Copyrights provide protection for works of original expression, including things such as text, photographs, illustrations, music, and other artistic and aesthetic works.

Protection is automatic and instantaneous just as soon as a copyrightable work is fixed in a tangible medium of expression. Although a copyright owner who wants to take advantage of the full range of protections available under U.S. law can make use of a copyright notice and registration of their copyright claim with the U.S. Copyright Office, neither is required. (But see *Reasons to Register* at the end of this chapter.)

The copyright rights vest in the author upon fixation, with or without them.

The copyright owner's exclusive rights include the right to:

- reproduce the work
- prepare derivative works based on the copyrighted work
- distribute copies of the work
- display the work publicly
- perform the work publicly
- in the case of sound recordings, distribute the work by digital transmission

The exercise of any of these rights without authorization from the copyright owner constitutes copyright infringement (unless it is excused under one of the recognized exceptions).

It's important to remember, though, that copyright law provides protection only for authorship or expression—that is, for creative combinations of words, images, and sounds, not for the underlying facts or ideas. The thinking here is that people shouldn't be able to appropriate mere concepts or historical facts to their exclusive use simply by being the first to articulate or report them. Facts, statistics, and concepts can be copied and republished without permission (though you may nonetheless wish to cite the source for support or credibility; and if you are writing scholarly work, your scholarly integrity will depend upon proper attribution).

What you cannot do is copy the creative manner in which the original facts or ideas were described or explained.

The unprotectability of facts and ideas gives rise to an underappreciated distinction between paraphrasing and plagiarism. The word *paraphrase* (derived from the Greek *para phrasien*, to show alongside) means, in its proper sense, to extract unprotected facts from protected expression—a perfectly honorable endeavor. The word plagiarize, on the other hand (from the Latin *plagiare*, to kidnap), means to appropriate someone else's literary composition and pass it off as one's own.

But if extracting facts and ideas is permissible, how do you separate them from the expression in which they are found?

For fact-based works, names, dates, places, and events—answers to the journalist's questions who, what, when, where, how, and why—are fair game.

Literary devices and techniques, conversely, belong to the creators and are off-limits. As a general rule, these and other kinds of protected expression may not be "reproduced"—that is to say, quoted, adapted, abridged, excerpted, traced, photocopied, or captured electronically—without permission.

Examples of such protected expression include all of the following:

Alliteration	Flashback	Personification
Allusion	Foreshadowing	Rhetorical question
Analogy	Hyperbole	Semantic Satiation
Assonance/consonance	Imagery	Simile
Colloquialism	Metaphor	Symbolism
Colorful Description	Oxymoron	Synecdoche
Euphemism	Paradox	Tautology
Exaggeration	Pathetic Fallacy	

Table 1.1

So a 200-word newspaper account about the appointment of a new member to a corporate board probably contains very little in the way of protected expression, but a 2,000-word human interest story or op-ed piece might contain very little in the way of unprotected fact.

Since the public's interest in free access to facts and ideas is not a factor with fiction, the scope of protection for it is much broader, encompassing not only the literal words but also the original plot lines and developed characters contained in them. Accordingly, if you are publishing a book about a celebrity who is principally known as a character in a film or television series, it is not enough to avoid including portions of the scripts. You must also be careful not to reproduce a description of the plot or of character traits that is so detailed that you have effectively appropriated a significant portion of the creator's labors.

EXAMINING EXCEPTIONS

Under some circumstances, expression protectable under copyright law may be freely available for use without permission. Perhaps the material lost its protection for failure to comply with the statutory prerequisites under prior U.S. law; perhaps it is excluded from copyright protection because it is a publication of the U.S. government; perhaps its term of protection has expired and it has entered the public domain for that reason or some other one.

Two decades ago U.S. law put conditions on copyright protection. Works first published prior to March 1, 1989, were required to carry a sufficient copyright notice, and any work that was published without satisfying this condition lost its copyright protection. If you are interested in quoting from a work that you know was published before this date, and if you have a complete, authorized copy that does not include a legally sufficient copyright notice, the work may be in the public domain.

Under current U.S. law, it is nearly impossible to lose copyright protection. A change in U.S. copyright law in 1989 eliminated the requirement of a copyright notice as a condition of copyright protection.

All works for which the statutory copyright period has expired are in the public domain. In the two decades prior to 1998, U.S. copyright law went through a series of changes that made the calculation of a work's copyright term an exercise in higher math. The cumulative effect of all these changes is that any work first published prior to 1923 is now necessarily in the public domain and may be freely copied or distributed. Works published after 1923 may also be in the public domain, but you can't assume that they are without a search of the U.S. Copyright

Office records to ascertain whether or not statutory renewals had been obtained on time. For example, a work first published between 1923 and 1963 for which an application to renew its copyright was not timely filed before the expiration of its first 28-year term lost out on its second term of protection and fell into the public domain upon the expiration of its first term (see Table 1.2).

When Copyright Expires

Creation/Publication Date	When Rights Vest	Term
Created on or after January 1, 1978	Upon fixation	Life plus 70 years (the term is defined differently for corporate, anonymous, and pseudonymous works)
Published before 1923	Copyrights have expired	None
Published from 1923 to 1963	When published with a legally sufficient copyright notice	28 years from publication plus an optional renewal upon application for 67 years
Published from 1964 to 1977	When published with a legally sufficient copyright notice	28 years from publication plus an automatic extension for 67 years

Table 1.2

Works that were created but unpublished as of 1978 are subject to a different set of requirements and may have a term of protection that extends to the year 2047 or beyond.

Publications of the federal government and its agencies are excluded by law from copyright protection. But the same is not true for works produced by state and local governments. And an essential element of the rule is that federal government documents must have been "authored" by the federal government. If someone under contract to the government writes a document and transfers or assigns the copyright to the government, then the government holds the copyright and you must get permission to copy or distribute the material.

And there are a number of exceptions to the monopoly rights otherwise vested in the copyright owner under certain specific circumstances set forth in U.S. copyright law, e.g., a preservation right for libraries and archives, a performance or display right in digital or face-to-face instruction or religious service, a right to back up or alter computer programs, the right to photograph or depict architectural works that are located in or accessible from public spaces, and so on.

CREATIVE COMMONS AND OPEN EDUCATIONAL RESOURCES

Copyright notwithstanding, some copyrighted work has been made available on fairly liberal terms so that request for permission is unnecessary. There are some people who believe intellectual property should be freely shared. For those people, a group called Creative Commons (CC) has developed an open licensing protocol that includes four basic forms of royalty free licenses (and some combinations of them): Attribution, ShareAlike, NonCommercial, and NoDerivatives.

- All four forms of Creative Commons licenses require that others who use a CC-licensed work in any way must give credit to the author in the way the author requests, but not in a way that suggests the author endorses them or their use. In the Attribution license, this is all that is required.
- In the ShareAlike license, the author allows others to copy, distribute, display, perform, and modify the

CC-licensed work, as long as they distribute any modified work on the same terms.
- In the NonCommercial license, the author allows others to copy, distribute, display, perform, and modify the CC-licensed work and use it for any purpose other than commercially.
- In the NoDerivatives license, the author allows others to copy, distribute, display, and perform only faithfully reproduced copies of your work.

Creative Commons provides HTML buttons to mark material that an author wishes to make available via one of the CC licenses.

Open Educational Resources (OER) consist of materials offered freely and openly for educators, students, and self-learners to use, reuse, and re-purpose for teaching, learning, and research. OER includes learning content, software tools to develop, use, and distribute content, and implementation resources such as open licenses. Much of OER is licensed under one or another of the Creative Commons licenses. But this distribution model is nascent and still evolving and so careful attention should be paid to the license terms associated with any OER resources.

SELF-PUBLISHED WORKS AND USE OF YOUR OWN WORK

It is now possible for authors to bypass traditional publishers and self-publish through a platform such as those offered by Amazon and Apple. In such cases, the author is required to accept the vendor's form contract before his/her work will be published. Under such contracts, the author generally keeps the copyrights in the work, grants to the vendor a non-exclusive distribution right, and agrees to some restrictions on format and pricing. Self-publishing does not necessarily preclude future publication with a traditional publisher, except in the case of academic and scholarly works.

If your work has been self-published, you may re-purpose it for other publications (provided that the publication at issue does not require previously unpublished work). If your work has been traditionally published, the terms of your publishing contract may preclude re-purposing your own work for other publications.

UNIVERSITY LICENSES

Some higher ed institutions have adopted policies under which they receive non-exclusive license of journal articles written by their faculty permitting the institution to post the articles on the internet and to allow certain noncommercial uses. The MIT Faculty Open Access Policy is an example: *https://libraries.mit.edu/scholarly/mit-open-access/open-access-policy/*. Such policies are at odds with the contracts of book and proprietary journal publishers and so amendments reconciling the two are required lest an author be in breach of the policy or the contract.

CAUTION FOR THOSE WRITING SCHOLARLY WORKS

Although copyright law does not provide protection for underlying facts and ideas, there are other principles at work that constrain what an author can take without attribution when it comes to scholarly, academic, and scientific writing. Publication in journals and monographs and other scholarly works is a means by which academics and scientists communicate the results of their research and build their reputations. Accordingly, whether or not copyright law would permit the re-use of facts or concepts without attribution, the policies of most scholarly institutions—universities, university presses, journals, and professional societies—require appropriate citation and attribution in writings that incorporate or build upon the discoveries or intellectual work product of others. More on this in Chapter 3.

REASONS TO REGISTER

The U.S. Copyright Office maintains a public catalog where you can register your claim of copyright in works authored or owned by you. Registration is permissive; it is not a condition of copyright protection. But some important advantages have been provided to encourage registration so that we have a more complete public record of who owns what:

- Registration puts the world on notice of your claim.
- Registrations obtained before infringement provide access to enhanced remedies, including the ability to recover your attorney's fees in an enforcement action and access to statutory damages of up to $150,000 per work infringed when the infringement is willful.
- Registrations secured within three months of first publication provide seamless access to those enhanced remedies retroactive to the date of first publication.
- Registrations secured within five years of first publication of your work are afforded a presumption of validity in court, making your proof case easier.
- Registrations can be filed with the U.S. Customs Service to block importation of infringing articles.
- Registration helps build and formalize a portfolio of intellectual property rights that can enhance the value of your business; facilitate financing, investment, or sale; and ease the due diligence burden for those transactions.

- Registration is inexpensive—currently $35 for online registration of a basic claim.

Also, although registration is not a condition of copyright protection, it is required before you can initiate a suit in federal district court. You can always wait until you decide to sue and register your claim at that time, but if you take this approach, you will lose access to the enhanced remedies and may lose access to the presumption of validity.

For more information and access to the searchable public catalog and online registration see *copyright.gov.*

② THE FAIR USE DEFENSE

THE FAIR USE DOCTRINE IS A COMPLEX RULE intended to protect the right of reasonable public access for certain limited purposes to works otherwise protected by copyright law.

The copyright statute says "fair use" of a copyrighted work without permission for purposes such as criticism, comment, news reporting, teaching, scholarship, or research is not an infringement of copyright. Whether the use is "fair" is determined by considering four factors:

(1) the purpose and character of the use, including whether it is of a commercial nature or is for nonprofit educational purposes
(2) the nature of the copyrighted work
(3) the amount and substantiality of the portion used in relation to the copyrighted work as a whole
(4) the effect of the use on the potential market for or value of the copyrighted work

A good example of the doctrine's application is the right of a book reviewer to quote passages from a book being reviewed without the consent of the book's author and for the purpose of illustrating comments and conclusions in the review. Quoting limited extracts from the published works of others for the purpose of analyzing, commenting on, or building upon their stated views or theories probably falls within the ambit of fair use. On the other hand, borrowing all or a substantial portion of a copyrighted work in order to avoid the necessity of creating or writing one is probably not within the scope of fair use and would require permission. Whether a given use is fair is a mixed question of law and fact determined by the courts, case by case, and considering in each instance each of the four factors. The endless variety of situations and circumstances that can be present in particular cases has precluded the formulation of exact rules in the statute and there is no legislative inclination to change this in light of the pace of technological change. While there are statutory provisions for library photocopying and legislatively endorsed guidelines for classroom copying, there are no statutory or case-law rules of thumb for most commercial purposes.

Under the first factor, the general rule has been that commercial uses are presumptively unfair. The idea is that if someone is profiting from the use of a copyrighted work, it should be the copyright holder. Nonprofit educational uses, on the other hand, cut in favor of a finding of fair use.

Under the second factor, the law provides greater access to works that are fact intensive or unavailable (e.g., out-of-print), because the point of copyright law is ultimately not to benefit the author but to "promote the progress of science and useful arts." (Article I, Section 8, Clause 8, U.S. Constitution). Unpublished works, conversely, get more protection because it is thought that the author should have the right to control the timing of publication and distribution of her/his work.

With respect to the third factor, a rumor, persistent among publishers and authors, has it that the law does provide for a word-count safe harbor—some say 300 words is the limit, some say 500, some say 1,000, some say 10 percent. Wherever these notions come from, none of them is grounded in fact. There is no particular number of words or pages that automatically qualifies as fair use. The focus here is instead on whether or not the amount used is more than is necessary to achieve the protected purpose.

At one time, the fourth factor (the effect of the use on the value of the source work) was considered the most important of the four factors. In recent decades, attention in many fair use cases has focused on the first factor and, in particular, whether the accused use is transformative. That is, does the accused work make a use that alters the source work with new expression, meaning, or message? For example, capturing and storing low resolution thumbnail images of photographs for the purpose of creating a searchable digital index is transformative in that the low resolution thumbnails are not an adequate substitute for the high-resolution originals and they do serve a purpose, indexing, not served by the originals.

A few litigated cases illustrate the interplay among the four factors.

In *Salinger v. Random House*, 200 words from the unpublished letters of J.D. Salinger directly quoted in an unauthor-ized biography were deemed to exceed the bounds of fair use, largely as a result of the unpublished character of the original letters.

Harper & Row v. Nation Enterprises, 300 words from a book quoted in a magazine article published prior to the release of the book were deemed outside the scope of fair use, in part because the unauthorized publication scooped the book publisher and undermined the value of the first serial rights to the book.

At the other end of the spectrum lies *Maxtone-Graham v. Burtchaell*, where 7,000 words from a pro-choice document about unwanted pregnancies were quoted in a pro-life work critical of its analysis and conclusions. The *Maxtone-Graham* court first paid homage to the single, irrefutable rule of fair-use analysis, saying: "There are no absolute rules as to how much of a copyrighted work may be copied and still be considered fair use." Here the court was influenced by the motivation behind the second work, which was intended as scholarly or philosophical criticism and was not a purely commercial endeavor, in reaching the conclusion that this extensive use of material was within the scope of fair use.

MORE FAIR USE CASES

The U.S. Copyright Office maintains an index of fair use cases at: *https://www.copyright.gov/fair-use/*. The index includes summaries of a broad selection of fair use cases from all levels of the federal court system. The cases are sortable by federal circuit and by category or type of use (e.g., music, parody, text work, unpublished work, etc.). For each case included, there is a brief summary of the facts, the relevant questions presented, and the court's determination as to whether the contested use was fair.

Stanford University also maintains a useful web fair use resource at: *https://fairuse.stanford.edu/about/*. This site includes primary case law, statutes, regulations, as well as current feeds of newly filed copyright lawsuits, pending legislation, regulations, copyright office news, scholarly articles, and blog and twitter feeds from practicing attorneys and law professors.

While each fair use case is decided on its own facts and no two cases are identical, searching these databases for cases involving circumstances similar to those confronting you in any given situation will give you some idea of how a court might analyze your situation in light of the four fair use factors and, ultimately, whether a court would be likely to find your use to be fair.

And although there are no bright line tests for most commercial purposes, there are some guidelines or best practices that, while not having the force of law do carry some weight in limited situations.

PRACTICAL POINTERS AND GUIDELINES

1) In the absence of any bright-line test, what can we infer from these and other fair use cases?

- Fact-based, nonfiction, or scientific works receive less protection than fictional works, and commercial works will probably be given less protection than literary or artistic works.
- Commercial uses are accorded less deference than uses that have a significant noncommercial purpose.
- Tables and charts containing facts can be copyrightable to the extent that the arrangement of information is original or creative (the facts are fair game, but the manner of display may not be).
- If you plan to use material you believe was published by a federal agency, you need to check for a copyright notice. If there is no copyright notice on the document, it is reasonable to assume that it is authored by the government and is in the public domain.

2) If you are quoting or copying without permission in reliance upon fair use:

- Transcribe accurately from the original.
- Provide proper attribution to the source (your credit line should say "Source:... " or "As reported in..." and not "Adapted from...." or "Reprinted with permission from...").
- Take only as much as you need for a permitted purpose—criticism, comment, news reporting, scholarship, teaching, or research.
- Avoid segregating the quoted material in a sidebar or box, particularly if you have appropriated the material simply to add illustration or color and as a substitute for creating an illustration or example.

- Make your use of quoted material transformative—that is, work it into the context of what you are otherwise saying and add some value by the use of criticism, comparison, or comment.

Bottom line: As difficult as it can be to know for certain whether the use you propose is fair, simply getting close may be good enough—the lack of certainty affects defendants and plaintiffs with equal force. Because U.S. copyright law gives a court the discretion to award fees to a defendant who prevails, a plaintiff who isn't certain of a win risks not only the loss of the case but also the unhappy possibility of having to pay the lawyers on both sides. (In 2004, Mattel was assessed nearly $2 million in fees for overzealous prosecution of an infringement claim in the face of a sound fair-use defense.)

Arguably, publishers and authors have not only a right but an obligation to defend First Amendment free speech and free press rights by making constant and vigorous use of the fair use defense—a malleable doctrine that has evolved over time and that is constantly challenged by the forces of changing technology and media.

CAUTION FOR THOSE WRITING SCHOLARLY WORKS

Fair use is a useful tool for trade and textbook authors. But for scholarly writers, although it may save you from having to get copyright permission for your incorporation of others' dis-coveries or concepts in your writing, you will still have to be careful to provide appropriate attribution. More on this in Chapter 3.

③ AVOIDING THE NEED TO SECURE PERMISSION

MAYBE IT WAS SOMETHING YOU SAW IN A MAGAZINE OR AT A BOOKstore. Maybe it was something you saw online. Maybe it was something that caught your eye in a grant application or proposal… a good idea in poorly skilled hands seemingly not up to the task. In any event, wherever you first saw it, it inspired you to develop and publish your own article or book on the subject.

Anyone who has worked in an intellectual or creative endeavor knows that many new works build to one degree or another on the earlier work of others. But getting a head start by leveraging the intellectual work product of another is potentially problematic. When does inspiration cross over into infringement or a breach of scholarly integrity? The lawyer's answer is: it depends.

It depends on how you obtained access to the source material. It depends on whether the source material is fiction or fact-heavy. It depends on what, and on how much, you took from the source material. And it depends on the nature and purpose of your writing.

You can be inspired by and reuse ideas, facts, or style of another's earlier work to form a new work without infringing a copyright. This is because these elements of a work are not protected by copyright—not "owned" by the copyright holder—and thus they are available to be reused and recast into new original expression. What is protected is the manner of expression—the author's analysis or interpretation of events, the way she structures the material and marshalls facts, the choice of words, the emphasis on particular events. (See Chapter 1, "First Things First: Parsing Copyright Protection".)

AMISTAD—A CASE IN POINT

The Amistad dispute was a case in point. La Amistad was a Spanish schooner being used to transport kidnapped Africans into slavery in the US in the summer of 1839. The Africans revolted en route and took control of the ship, but were captured before they could complete their escape and were subsequently put on trial. Their case went to the US Supreme Court, which ultimately set them free. The story of their revolt, capture, and trial has been depicted in a play, a historical novel, *Echo of Lions*, and a Steven Spielberg movie, *Amistad*.

No one can own history simply by being first to write about it. But in this case, gaps in the historical record were filled by the book author with fictional scenes and characters in her book, published in 1989. Production of the Spielberg movie was announced in 1996. One year later, the book author sued, claiming that the Spielberg movie appropriated nine of those gap-filling inventions and embellishments.

The California district court hearing the case noted that, because both the book and the movie were based on historical events, the plot, settings, and sequence of events were inherently similar. The court observed,

> further, that the dialogue was not similar and that the mood and pace were also different. Ultimately, the court was not convinced that the nine gap-filling inventions and embellishments claimed by the book author to have been copied by Spielberg actually involved protectable expression.

But having to defend a case, even if you prevail in the end, is expensive and distracting. What do you need to know, and what steps should you take to avoid or prepare yourself to respond to a claim, with an eye toward keeping it from ever getting to litigation?

THE POTENTIAL CLAIMS

First, you should understand the nature of the potential claims because the circumstances that give rise to each of them, the available remedies, and the defensive steps you would take differ. The most likely claim is for copyright infringement, i.e., a claim that you took more than you should have from someone else's copyrighted work. The other, less likely, claim is for breach of a contract implied in fact or in law. This claim is not dependent on your having taken too much copyrighted expression, but instead is focused on how you got access to the book idea and whether it was under circumstances that created a reasonable expectation of compensation for any exploitation.

COPYRIGHT INFRINGEMENT

Copyright is not a single right but is instead a bundle of rights that belong exclusively to the copyright owner. One of those rights is the reproduction right—so you cannot make a verbatim copy of someone else's copyrighted work without their consent. But another one of those exclusive rights is the adaptation right—

the right to adapt a work or make derivatives of it. Accordingly, copying does not have to be verbatim to be infringing.

If you have had access to a copyrighted work and if you then prepare a similar work on the same or a similar subject, you have opened the door to a copyright infringement claim—a claim that your work is an unauthorized derivative of the source work, i.e., that you started with a copy of the source work and, although you may have made changes to it or added to it work of your own, the resulting work still includes a material amount of protected expression from the original.

Importantly, copying is an essential element of copyright infringement. Sometimes there is direct evidence of copying—an admission, or a witness, or some unique turn of phrase or other element reproduced in the accused work that could not have gotten there other than by copying. But more often copying must be established by circumstantial evidence—evidence of access to the original coupled with an accused work that is so similar to the subject work that the similarities are unlikely to have been coincidental. Thus, evidence of access plus substantial similarity permits an inference of copying.

THE CIRCUMSTANTIAL CASE

The stronger and more compelling the evidence of access, the less similarity is required to support the inference of copying. In the Amistad case, there was evidence that the book was pitched to the person who subsequently became the script writer for the Spielberg movie. But evidence that a book was published and widely distributed and promoted can also serve as evidence that access was more likely than not.

Copying must be established on two levels. First, it must be established as a fact. This step permits consideration of the similarity of both unprotected and protected elements. But in order to establish actionable infringement, the copying must have included a material amount of protected expression—literary devices, plot devices, scenes, character descriptions, and the like.

Although similarity of reported facts and ideas— answers to the journalist's questions of who, what, when, where, and why—can help to establish copying as a matter of fact, this by itself will not be infringing without evidence also of appropriation of protected expression. For this reason, fact-heavy works are generally accorded less protection than works of fiction.

For works of fiction, the public's interest in free access to facts and ideas is absent, and thus the scope of protection is much broader, encompassing not only the literal words on paper but also the original plot lines and well-developed characters contained therein. Thus, if you are producing a book about a celebrity who is principally known for the character he/she plays in a film or television series, it is not enough that you avoid including portions of the scripts from the film/series. You must also be careful that you do not reproduce in your book so detailed a description of the plot or character traits from the film/series that you have effectively appropriated a significant portion of the producer's creative labors.

There are no bright line tests here. The circumstantial case is just that—circumstantial. It is based on establishment of certain premises that permit the court or the jury to infer that they are connected in a particular way. The final decision about whether each of the necessary premises has been established and to what extent and about whether the combination of them is strong enough to permit the inference of actionable copying is unavoidably subjective. The final outcome can almost never be predicted with absolute confidence. But if, by following the best practices set out below, you can at least make it a close question, then you will have reduced the likelihood of a fee award in favor of the plaintiff even if he/she were to be successful and this circumstance will often make litigation economically unviable.

BREACH OF IMPLIED CONTRACT

Altogether apart from the potential for a copyright claim as described above, there is also under certain circumstances the potential for a claim not dependent upon the unauthorized appropriation of protected expression. Where you obtained access to the subject work under circumstances that might create a reasonable expectation in the minds of the parties that the subject work would only be exploited by the recipient in exchange for compensation, there may be a breach of implied contract claim. Accepting and reviewing a query or proposal, whether solicited or unsolicited, may give rise to such an expectation. These "submission-of-idea" claims are creatures of state law, the elements of which vary from state to state. Some states require that the submitted idea be absolutely novel (i.e., not previously known to anyone other than the discloser). Some require only that it was not already known to the recipient.

PRACTICAL POINTERS AND GUIDELINES

Recognizing, as we noted at the start of this chapter, that most creative work is inspired by the earlier work of others, there are some best practices that you can adopt yourself that will put you in a position to deflect or defend against claims that your work borrows impermissibly from the earlier works of others.

1) Consult a number of sources, not one, and keep a list of the works you consult. Someone said it: Copying from one source is infringement; copying from multiple sources is research. It's not literally true, of course. It is certainly possible to infringe multiple works in one project. But to the extent that you have a record of having consulted multiple works and to the extent that the cited similarities

between your work and an accuser's work are also present in some or all of the other works you consulted, it will be less likely that those similarities will support an inference that you copied impermissibly from any one of them.

2) Take skeletal notes... just the facts and abstract ideas, and keep these notes. Working through this intermediate step will make it less likely for you to pick up protected expression from a source work inadvertently. It is not uncommon for a writer to take detailed notes from source materials, set them aside for other projects, and return to them months or years later, having lost track of where they came from or how closely they were copied or paraphrased. Also, to support your memory, if you are doing scholarly work, record the source (author and publication) for each concept or finding in your notes for attribution later.

3) Set the source works aside and work from your notes. This will help you avoid inadvertent appropriation of protected expression.

4) Keep a contemporaneous log of your writing activities and how much time you spend developing your manuscript (the less time it takes you, the more likely it is that you took inappropriate short cuts). The contemporaneous notes are business records admissible as evidence in support of your recollections about how your work was created. And evidence that you took these precautions and that you did not generate your manuscript in an unreasonably short period of time will help you defeat an inference that your work was the result of impermissible copying.

5) Keep your interim drafts, for the same reason.

6) Saul Bellow said it: "You never have to change anything you got up in the middle of the night to write." And I think it's safe to say that whatever wakes you in the night and moves you to start writing is very likely sufficiently removed from whatever inspired you to make infringement unlikely as both a practical matter and a legal matter. For everything else, watch your step.
7) If your work is online and the work you wish to extract is also online, consider linking to the work you'd like to reference. Linking merely directs your reader to the third-party material at its source and does not result in an exercise of any of the rights belonging exclusively to the copyright holder. It also supplies unassailable attribution since your source is fully disclosed.

ATTRIBUTION, AUTHORSHIP, AND SCHOLARLY INTEGRITY

Altogether apart from the question of whether your reference to the work of some other requires you to get copyright permission, you may nonetheless need to provide appropriate attribution or even authorship credit if your writing is for a scholarly, scientific, or academic publication.

Scholarship involves becoming familiar with the existing body of work, the work of others, and adding your own original thought. Ideas have value. When you acknowledge the work of others, you give credit where it is due, you increase the cogency of your own work, and you equip your audience to examine your contributions against what has come before. Scholarly integrity requires that you not claim origination or authorship for the work of others, that you attribute their work when you have incorporated and built upon it, that you not claim authorship for work to which you did not materially contribute, and that you share authorship with all who have contributed materially to a work you have participated in creating.

Any verbatim use of text from a third-party work, no matter how large or small the quotation should be clearly attributed. Direct quotations must be placed in quotation marks or indented beyond the regular margin. The quotation should be accompanied, either within the text or in a footnote, by a precise indication of the source, identifying the author, title, and page numbers. Even if you use only a short phrase, you must use quotation marks in order to set off the borrowed language from your own and cite the source.

More significant contributions suggest a co-authorship credit. These contributions can be in the design or conduct of research, analysis of research results or data, or composition of the text describing the results. Supervision of research or writing alone is not generally sufficient to entitle a faculty member to claim co-authorship credit for student work. Where the line between attribution and co-authorship is otherwise drawn depends to some extent on the field in which you are writing.

In medicine and the social sciences, in order to earn authorship credit one must have contributed substantially to the conception and design of the study, drafted or critically reviewed the article, and stand accountable for all aspects of the work. In natural sciences, mathematics, computer science, and physics, research involvement is less critical and material involvement in the drafting of the article is the driver.

Note that authorship for copyright purposes is a different matter with different consequences. From a copyright standpoint, the human being who creates a work of original expression is deemed to be the author and owner of the copyrights in that work from the moment it is fixed in a tangible medium. There is, however, an important exception to this default rule. Copyrightable works that are created by an employee within the scope of his/her duties as an employee are said to be "for-hire" and in this case it is the employer who is deemed the author and owner of the work for copyright purposes. Higher ed faculty are generally employed by their institutions and a part of what is expected of them is that they write and publish. So you might think that their scholarly writing would fall into this "for-hire" category. But there is a competing interest at work here—academic freedom. Higher ed institutions do not direct what their faculty write, and generally don't want to be responsible for it either. So most have adopted formal written policies that disclaim any ownership interest in the scholarly writing of their faculty. According to the AAUP Statement on Copyright, "it has been the prevailing academic practice to treat the faculty member as the copyright owner of works that are created independently and at the faculty member's own initiative for traditional academic purposes." When it comes to software development and curriculum design or work that is institution-directed or assigned, however, there is less uniformity from institution to institution and it is important to refer to the intellectual property policies of each institution to ascertain who owns what. When it comes to co-authorship, here, too, there are differences between what copyright law provides and permits on the one hand, and what considerations of scholarly integrity will allow on the other. Under the default provisions of copyright law, co-authors share an undivided pro-rata share of the ownership interests in the work they have co-authored. If there are two co-authors, they each have an undivided 50% interest in the entire work (not just an interest in their contributions); if there are three co-authors, they each have a 33.3% interest in the entire work, and so on. Any co-author is free to make any non-exclusive use of the work that co-author wishes, without the consent of his/her co-authors.

Here, the rules of academia depart significantly. Publication is the Holy Grail in academic life. The prestige of the journal in which one is published is of vital importance. Once an article, or a variation or extract of it, has been published, it will not generally be considered for publication by any other journal. Accordingly, publication in a journal or by a press selected by one co-author without the consent and participation of all co-authors is a serious breach of trust and would very likely result in censure, loss of tenure, or other adverse consequence for the accused.

4 DEFAMATION PRIMER

As stated in the introduction to this book, an author's First Amendment freedom is bounded by certain limits, including an obligation to be careful with the facts. And, if you consider the recent history of U.S. libel litigation, it appears that book publishers have been generally better about this than their other media brethren.

The Media Law Resource Center (MLRC) is a professional association of media companies and their lawyers that has been collecting and analyzing information on trials and verdicts involving the defense of media companies' First Amendment rights for more than three decades. Over this period, MLRC has examined nearly 600 trial verdicts and the conclusions it has drawn are enlightening.

WHAT DO THE NUMBERS TELL US?

Across all forms of media, the media companies lose at trial in approximately 60% of the cases, but many of these unfavorable judgments are subsequently reversed or reduced so that the plaintiffs hold onto their entire award in only about 20% of the cases. Juries are evidently overly sympathetic to plaintiffs whose reputations have been sullied, but the trial judges and appellate courts moderate this bias.

The vast majority of the cases tried to verdict involve newspapers; a much smaller number involve magazines; and very few involve books (and in all three categories the number of cases has steadily decreased over the past 30 years). That newspapers are the most frequent targets makes intuitive sense—the newsworthy topics they cover are more often likely to provoke an angry response and the time from discovery to publication is necessarily shorter than that for magazines or books, allowing less opportunity for fact checking.

But it may also be the case that simple economics is equally at work in driving this pattern. A newspaper defending against a libel claim is essentially defending its ability to report the news; it's defending its entire business. A book publisher, on the other hand, is more often protecting its right to continue distribution of a single title. Consequently, it is likely that the book cases settle early and never make it to verdict as the profit to be made on a single book would not often justify the cost and risk associated with a libel trial to verdict. The cost of such a defense will almost certainly be into six figures and MLRC reports that the median award is $100K, with 45% of the cases resulting in verdicts north of $1MM in the last couple of years. Even where a media perils insurance policy is available to provide coverage, the deductible will probably leave the publisher to bear the first $50-$100K or more of expense.

WHAT ARE THE ELEMENTS OF A LIBEL CLAIM?

Defamation is an umbrella term that encompasses both libel and slander—essentially false allegations that damage a person's reputation. Libel is defamation in written or other recorded form. Slander, on the other hand, concerns oral and otherwise transitory statements and is less often at issue for authors and publishers.

The law of defamation in the U.S. is primarily state-based, so the technical elements of a defamation claim will vary from state to state. Generally speaking, however, in order to recover on a defamation claim, a plaintiff must establish each and every one of the following:

(1) an unprivileged publication
(2) of a defamatory statement of fact
(3) that is false,
(4) that is of and concerning a living plaintiff,
(5) that causes damage to the plaintiff's reputation, and
(6) that is made with the requisite degree of fault (at least negligence).

Publication occurs if at least one other person besides the plaintiff reads the defamatory statement. When a book or journal is distributed for sale to the public at large, whether in print or e-book form, the "publication" element is necessarily satisfied.

A *defamatory* statement is one that has any tendency to injure an individual or entity in their trade or profession, that has a tendency to lower their reputation in the community, or that exposes them to public scorn, contempt, or ridicule.

A *false* statement is one that is not substantially true. Most courts do not require one hundred percent accuracy, but do require that the gist of the statement be true. A materially true statement cannot give rise to a defamation action; the law of defamation is designed to address only false statements affecting the reputation of a person or entity.

Note that, when dealing with falsity, a court will not dismiss a defamation action simply because it is literally true if it is not also substantively true. For example, correctly repeating a defamatory statement properly attributed to another source, as: "according to John Doe, Jane Doe is an alcoholic," does not permit the defendant to shift responsibility for a defamation claim to the source. *This is true even if John Doe in fact made the statement at issue.* If the truth is that Jane is not an alcoholic, the publisher of John's statement can still be found liable. Thus all statements (both direct and indirect) should be appropriately fact-checked prior to publication.

A *statement of fact* is fairly self-explanatory: only factual, or allegedly factual, statements can form the basis of a defamation action. A fact is something that is or could be empirically verified. Opinion, conversely, is protected by the First Amendment free speech and free press guarantee. Statements of pure opinion generally cannot give rise to a defamation action. In determining whether a statement is fact or opinion, courts typically ask four questions:

1) Is the statement capable of being proved true or false?
2) What is the journalistic context of the statement? Is the statement made as part of a fictional account or in a work of commentary, or is it found in a non-fiction work or an exposé.
3) What is the social context of the statement? Is the statement being made as part of a political debate?
4) What is the ordinary meaning of the words used?

The *of and concerning* element of a defamation claim requires that any statement alleged to be defamatory be about an identifiable plaintiff who is still living at the time the claim is brought. This means that someone other than the plaintiff must be able to identify the plaintiff as the subject of the statement— it is not enough that the plaintiff alone can tell the statement refers to them. Conversely, fictionalizing or disguising the name of the subject will not eliminate exposure if the subject is nonetheless identifiable from the facts and circumstances otherwise disclosed. Remember that a person may be identified in many ways, including name, nickname, photograph, job title, address, familial relationship, and so on. And it is not necessary that *you* be able to recognize them from what is disclosed, only that one other be able to recognize them.

The right not to be defamed is a personal right as opposed to a property right. The focus of defamation law is on injury to reputation. The deceased have no reputation to protect and so defamation claims expire on the death of the plaintiff and so cannot be pursued by the heirs or personal representatives of the decedent.

Additionally, the plaintiff must have suffered *damage* as a result of the publication of any allegedly defamatory statement. In some circumstances, damages are presumed—we call this libel per se and accusation of a crime is one example. In other circumstances, the plaintiff must be able to prove that, in fact, his, her or its reputation was harmed by the defendant's publication. Objective indicia of this type of damage include testimony from former colleagues and/or friends that those individuals now think less of the plaintiff as a direct result of the defendant's publication; evidence that the plaintiff was terminated from his or her job as a result of defendant's publication; evidence that the plaintiff is unable to secure business or employment as a result of the publication; and similar evidence showing that the plaintiff's standing in the community has been affected by the publication or that he/she is being ostracized or shunned. Provided the plaintiff can produce sufficient evidence, he or she is also entitled to damages for humiliation suffered and emotional distress.

Eliminate any one of the foregoing elements and the claim fails. Anonymize the story, make sure the facts are substantially true, or at least make sure that you have taken appropriate care to check your facts (even if they later turn out to have been wrong), and you have reduced or eliminated the risk of a bad result.

WHAT IS THE REQUIRED DEGREE OF FAULT?

Libel is not a strict liability claim in the U.S. The First Amendment has been interpreted to require at least a showing of negligence where the subject of the alleged libel is a private figure. However, if the subject is instead a public figure or public official, the First Amendment imposes a heavier burden on him/her in establishing defamation, this in deference to the public's interest in free and open discourse about controversial and newsworthy subjects. Nearly all movie, television, music, political, and sports celebrities will be considered public figures in the eyes of the law.

There are two types of public figures: (1) general purpose public figures and (2) limited purpose public figures. A general-purpose public figure is one who has achieved general fame or notoriety. A limited purpose public figure is, by contrast, one who has injected himself/herself into a particular public debate in an effort to affect the outcome of that debate.

A public figure or public official plaintiff must establish that the defendant acted with "actual malice" in publishing the defamatory statement. Acting with actual malice means publishing the statements at issue *with knowledge of their falsity, or with reckless disregard as to the truth or falsity of the state-ment*. What constitutes reckless disregard will vary depending on the circumstances of a particular case.

LIBEL TOURISM HAZARDS

U. S. publishers, accustomed to First Amendment free press protections, have been caught off guard in recent years by less press-friendly libel laws in other countries and by just how easy it is for a would-be plaintiff to travel in search of one of these more favorable forums willing to exercise jurisdiction—a tactic sometimes referred to as "libel tourism."

Early cases of libel tourism involved a Saudi businessman, Sheikh Khalid bin Mahfouz, who was accused in a number of publications of involvement in financing international terrorism. Mahfouz, though a citizen of Saudi Arabia, traveled to England to pursue his accusers, where he took advantage of the very low bar set for libel plaintiffs under English law to sue or threaten to sue at least 29 times.

A quick comparison of English and U.S. libel law explains Mahfouz's move:

- In England, the publisher-defendant has to prove that the published statement at issue is true. In the U.S., the initial burden is on the plaintiff to introduce proof of falsity.
- Opinion is not protected in England, as it is in the U.S. This compounds the impact of the publisher's initial burden, which becomes proving that its opinion is substantively true.
- In England, parody and satire are not protected forms of speech as they are in the U.S.
- The publisher is liable without regard to fault in England. In the U.S., the burden is on the plaintiff to prove, at a minimum, that the publisher acted negligently, and in some cases that the publisher acted with actual malice.

Little wonder then that English libel plaintiffs win more than 98% of the cases they bring.

And it is relatively easy for an English court to exercise jurisdiction. In the case of Mahfouz, an academic book written and published in the U.S. was subjected to suit in England because just 23 copies of it had been sold into England via amazon.com.

England is not the worst place for a publisher to face a libel claim. In many European countries, the dead can be libeled (in the U.S., libel law is limited to protecting the reputations of the living). In other countries, such as Senegal and Thailand, libel has been criminalized so that a publisher might be jailed (or worse), and a single copy of an accused work purchased via the internet for shipment to these countries—or the download there of even a single e-book—will subject its publisher to exposure.

The good news is that a judgment overseas will not necessarily have much impact on you unless you sometimes travel to the relevant country or have assets there (such as consigned inventory or royalty receivables).

There was a time when you also had to worry about a foreign judgment being domesticated and enforced in the U.S. But as a consequence of, and a partial solution to, libel tourism, both houses of the U.S. Congress unanimously voted to enact a federal law making foreign libel judgments unenforceable in U.S. courts where domestic enforcement of the foreign judgment would offend U.S. notions of free speech and press.

The (SPEECH) Act (for Securing the Protection of our Enduring and Established Constitutional Heritage) was signed into U.S. law by President Barack Obama in 2010. Just one year later, the first case granting declaratory relief under the act resulted in insulating a U.S. defendant from domestic enforcement of a Canadian libel judgment.

THE RIGHT-TO-BE-FORGOTTEN RISKS

U.S. publishers are often surprised to discover that a right to be forgotten has developed in some countries and is evolving in others. Where this right is recognized, true but unflattering historical events that would be fair game for publication under U.S. law may be shielded in ways that hamper publication of some biographies or books about sensational past events.

Although publication of historical facts is protected by the first amendment in the U.S., a right to have true but embarrassing information shielded from publication exists in other jurisdictions, notably Germany, England, France, Spain, and perhaps soon the whole European Union.

An early case with U.S. implications involved two German

men implicated in the sensational murder of a German actor in 1990. The two men, half-brothers Wolfgang Werlé and Manfred Lauber, were convicted of the crime, served their sentences in a German prison, and were released in 2007 and 2008. An English language Wikipedia article described the crime and named the convicted killers, notwithstanding German law that allows a criminal's name to be withheld from publication once the criminal has served a prison term.

In 2009, lawyers for Werlé sued the Wikimedia Foundation in Germany to have the article withdrawn, citing a 1973 German court decision that allows the suppression of a criminal's name in news accounts once he is released from custody. They obtained a default judgment there, but they have not been able to enforce it in the U.S.

FICTION/FACTION DANGERS

Two of the essential elements of a libel claim are that the accused defamatory statement must be an assertion of an actual fact and that it must be about a real, living, and identifiable person. Accordingly, one would think that works of fiction would be immune from libel claims. After all, a work of fiction is, by definition, a product of the author's imagination and it is not held out to be either factual or about real, living people.

But fiction is often inspired by an author's experiences (sometimes too closely) and literature is full of instances of offended authors getting even with their real-life oppressors by casting them in unflattering or unsavory roles. When that happens, what is presented as fiction moves away from the truly imaginary and crosses over into the more risky territory sometimes referred to as "faction."

Whenever a work labeled fiction can be reasonably read as stating actual facts about a real person, courts allow juries to decide whether the work conveys defamatory meaning (and we know what happens when these cases are allowed to go to the jury in the U.S.).

A case brought in Illinois in 1996 concerned a short story published in *Seventeen* magazine as a part of a group of stories titled *New Voices in Fiction*. The story's author, a native of southern Illinois, wrote in the first person about a high-school classmate named Bryson and described her in the story as a "platinum-blond, blue-eye-shadowed, faded-blue-jeaned, black polyester-topped shriek" who lives "on the other side of town" and who participated in certain specified unchaste (or words to that effect) behavior.

As it happens, there actually *was* a young woman named Bryson who had gone to high school in southern Illinois, and when she sued, claiming that readers who knew her would reasonably recognize this short story as a false and defamatory allegation about her, the Illinois court decided that she was right, even though the story had been characterized as fiction.

There was no discussion in the court's opinion about whether the author and the real Ms. Bryson attended high school together or whether they even knew each other (presumably because they didn't). As one commentator said, what matters is not who is aimed at, but rather who is hit. So the intent of the author may go into the mix, but it is not determinative and an absence of intent will not save author or publisher if a reasonable reader perceives a defamatory meaning.

There are at least two strategies for avoiding faction-type libel claims. One focuses on dissuading potential plaintiffs from stepping forward, and the other focuses on effective use of a disclaimer.

To dissuade potential plaintiffs from suing, an author might imbue a character based on a real person with some physical or mental defect or some potently humiliating attribute so that no self-respecting person would choose to identify with the character by complaining. Michael Crichton reportedly used this tactic after he was offended by a critical profile written by a *New Republic* columnist. Crichton's next novel included a character with a name nearly identical to Michael Crowley who, like Crowley, graduated from Yale and was a political journalist in D.C. But the character was cast as a pedophile (with certain specified anatomical features correspondingly child-like). No claim was ever advanced.

The disclaimer strategy relies less on human vanity and more on a straightforward message calculated to explain the limited purpose for which real places or events have been employed and to dispel absolutely the potential for any reader reasonably to read in a defamatory meaning about a real, living person.

For example, in writing a novel that delivers a social commentary on past practices in the institutionalized treatment of the infirm and insane, an author might choose to draw on real places and events to lend credence to the story and the publisher would make it unequivocally clear in cover copy and promotional materials that the work is a novel.

The publisher of such a novel would be well advised also to include an explanation like the following as a prominent element of the front matter:

> *An Important Note to Readers*
> *The [Name] State Institute for the Feeble Minded was a real place in [Name] County, [State]. It existed at a time in our history when accepted notions about what constituted a disability, how to care for the disabled, what they might be capable of accomplishing, and even what to call them were very different than they are today. Many of the places and historical events in this book are real and help to anchor the story. But the characters and events depicted, though inspired by the people who endured that era, have been fictionalized for dramatic effect. Names, characters, places, and incidents have been altered and molded by the author's imagination and are neither represented nor intended to be a literal account*

of people or events. Though the story may be evocative of certain actual events, locales, or persons, living and dead, the details are fiction and not fact.

PROTECTION POSSIBILITIES

Apart from being mindful of the increased risk when your books travel, being careful with your facts, and being crystal clear about the line between fact and fiction, there are a few other things to keep in mind as you work to manage your risk for libel claims.

Consider, for example, retractions. Usually thought of in connection with newspapers and other serial publications because of opportunities they offer to correct or amplify content in a later issue, retractions can have some impact in book publishing through reprints and errata sheets.

If, despite your careful attention, a libel claim finds its way to your desk, the prompt offer of a correction in the next printing —or, in some cases, in an errata sheet made immediately available to libraries and distributors and inserted into existing stock— can go a long way toward defusing tensions and reducing the likelihood of litigation.

An offer of retraction has psychological impact as a demonstration of empathy and contrition, but retractions can also have legal impact. This varies from state to state. In some states, the fact that a retraction was offered or published is admissible inmitigation of damages or to establish a lack of malice. In at least one state, a potential plaintiff's demand for a retraction may be a prerequisite to filing suit. Some state statutes purport to require publication of a timely served demand for retraction, though provisions like that are generally thought to be unconstitutional as compelled speech.

So your opportunities to use retractions to good effect will be determined by where you are located or where you are likely to be sued. Still, retraction is a tactic you should not overlook.

Media perils insurance is also worth attention. No matter how cautious you are, some libel exposures may not be evident until they are already at your door. For this reason and others, media perils insurance coverage should probably be part of almost every publisher's risk management plan.

PRACTICAL POINTERS AND GUIDELINES

1) Check, and re-check, your facts. You don't have to be perfect, but you can't be sloppy or careless or negligent.
2) Look for corroboration of allegations made by individuals who are quoted. Whether one source is enough will depend upon the severity of the allegation and the credibility of the source—statements by ex-spouses and discharged employees, for example, should be regarded skeptically. Remember that an accurate quotation does not absolve you of liability, although there may be separate privileges applicable to the accurate recitation of facts set forth, or statements made, in court documents and legislative and judicial proceedings, at least where the outcome is fairly reported.
3) Don't willfully disregard important facts, witnesses, or documents that may contradict the picture you want to create for the reader.
4) Conduct enough research and investigation into the statements you are going to publish to be convinced of the truth of those statements.
5) Note that just because a statement has been published before, by somebody else, does not mean you can safely republish it without risk. Each time a defamatory statement is published it can create a

whole new cause of action. Investigate the truth of all published statements, even the ones you can attribute to some other source.

6) Be extremely careful when publishing factual statements involving *private* individuals. Unlike public figures, private figures generally need only establish that you were *negligent* in publishing a false statement about them—not that you acted with actual malice. This is a lower standard that requires increased care.

7) Avoid exaggerating or sensationalizing facts. At some point you may actually change the meaning of an otherwise true statement and make it false.

8) Make sure your titles, subtitles, chapter titles, headings, and captions match, and do not go further than what is said in the accompanying text.

9) Not all false statements are readily recognizable as defamatory. Seemingly innocuous-looking statements can conflict with important personal or professional positions in ways you would not necessarily anticipate. Check all the facts, not just the obviously unflattering ones.

10) Getting a depiction release can go a long way toward eliminating exposure as well as solving other potential problems. When feasible (and it's obviously not feasible in an exposé or tell-all memoir or unauthorized biography), consider asking the subject to sign an agreement, sometimes called a depiction release, that provides for access and cooperation, that provides exclusive or first publication rights, and that releases privacy and defamation claims.

11) Be careful, when illustrating a story with stock photos to avoid suggesting, by the proximity of the image to the message, something defamatory (e.g., stock photo of a man and woman talking in an office used to illustrate an article about sexual harassment in the workplace).

5) PRIVACY PRIMER

THE LAW OF PRIVACY IS ALMOST ENTIRELY A CREATURE of state law. Accordingly, as with defamation, what constitutes an invasion of privacy can vary from state to state. Most states recognize four types of invasion of privacy:

(1) the publication of private facts about an individual;
(2) intrusion into an individual's seclusion;
(3) false light invasion of privacy; and
(4) misappropriation of the right of publicity.

All of the different types of invasion of privacy actions, with the exception of intrusion into seclusion, are premised on *publication* of information about an individual. Thus in any action brought by a plaintiff for an invasion of privacy, he/she will necessarily have to establish that there was some publication of information about them. When dealing with books and journals, again, this element is largely presumed.

And as is the case with defamation, privacy rights (except, in some states, the right of publicity) are personal rights and any claim expires with the death of the plaintiff. In about half the states, the right of publicity is treated as a property right and does survive the death of the subject. For more on this, see Chapter 6.

PUBLICATION OF PRIVATE FACTS

In addition to publication, a plaintiff seeking to establish an invasion of privacy based on publication of private facts has to establish all of the following:

- the information is truly *private* in nature;
- publication of that information would be *highly offensive* to a reasonable person; and
- the information is *not of legitimate public concern or interest.*

Only "private" information can form the basis of an invasion of privacy action. If particular information is already known by a significant segment of the public, it cannot, by definition, be considered private. Further, courts have consistently held that those activities that occur in public cannot be private in nature. Similarly, information contained in public records (court documents and the like) cannot be private in nature.

The requirement that the publication of information be "highly offensive to a reasonable person" means that it is not enough that the plaintiff was embarrassed by the publication. Rather, a jury must be able to determine that a *reasonable* person would also be *highly* offended by the publication. This requirement is consistent with recognition of the media's right to inform the public about truthful matters.

Finally, if the information is of legitimate concern to the public, there is no invasion of privacy based on publication. Courts have been fairly liberal in defining what is of legitimate public concern. Before publishing any particular private information, ask yourself, is this matter newsworthy? Although the universe of items that can be newsworthy may seem fairly broad, if you sense that material may be private, sensitive, or offensive, it is best to seek the advice of legal counsel.

INTRUSION INTO SECLUSION

Unlike the other types of invasion of privacy, intrusion into seclusion is not premised on the publication of information. Rather, it is premised on *the way a defendant gathers information.* Intrusion into seclusion is what most people think of when they think of the use of hidden cameras, hidden microphones, and wiretapping. But it can also include physical presence of a reporter or other individual into a private area, whether or not an actual trespass occurs.

Generally speaking, you have intruded into the seclusion of another if that individual had a "reasonable expectation of privacy" under the circumstances. As with the publication of private facts, an individual does not have a reasonable ex-pectation of privacy in a public place if others *could* see/ hear/observe the individual. Courts have consistently found no reasonable expectation of privacy in restaurants, common areas of shopping malls, and on public streets. In the workplace setting, however, it has been held that employees might expect co-employees to overhear them, but not expect that their conversations will be made public by the media.

FALSE LIGHT

In many states, publication of information that places an individual in a false light is actionable if

- the false light in which the individual is placed would be highly offensive to a reasonable person; and
- the defendant acted with the required degree of fault.

False light liability often arises in situations in which the press "dramatizes" the truth: when a purposeful distortion of true facts occurs in an effort to sensationalize a story. Liability can also arise when a defendant uses "file" photographs in support of an unrelated story.

Note once again the requirement that the publication be highly offensive to a reasonable person. This means, of course, that it is not necessarily sufficient for the plaintiff himself or herself to be embarrassed or offended by the publication. The jury must be able to determine that a reasonable person would be highly offended.

Although all states require some level of fault on the part of the defendant, there is no uniform level of fault required. For the most part, courts require that any plaintiff—whether a public figure or private individual—establish "actual malice" on the part of the defendant in order to recover.

PRACTICAL POINTERS AND GUIDELINES

1) Does the matter being published include any private facts about an individual? If so, you must determine that these are a legitimate matter of public interest (i.e., newsworthy) before you move forward with publication. Always ask whether the public has a legitimate interest in the matter at issue.
2) The more information is already widely known, the less it is likely to be considered "private" information. Information that has been previously published in magazines, newspapers, etc. is presumably no longer private.
3) Avoid the urge to sensationalize information. Sensationalism for sensationalism's sake can defeat the newsworthiness protection of your publication. Courts will protect the press's right to inform only when the information is legitimate.
4) When publishing photos along with your articles, make sure the photos are directly related to the content of the article.
5) Do not dramatize or distort facts. Doing so could lead to a false light claim.

6) When gathering information by means of hidden or hidden microphone, be careful to tape only in areas accessible to the general public. Remember that you can be found liable for intruding into a plaintiff's seclusion if they had a reasonable expectation of privacy under the circumstances.
7) Gathering personal information about an individual from their private records can constitute an intrusion into seclusion. Steer clear of such sources when gathering information.
8) Remember that stock photos from an agency may bring with them invasion of privacy problems. Do not assume that just because you acquired a photo from a stock agency that there is no problem with intrusion into seclusion or other invasion of privacy torts.
9) For purposes of intrusion, keep in mind that whether or not you publish the information, your mere presence or the presence of newsgathering equipment in a private place may lead to liability.
10) When in doubt regarding whether or not the publication of particular information may constitute an invasion of privacy, consult with your attorneys to minimize risk.

⑥ RIGHT OF PUBLICITY

MISAPPROPRIATION OF AN INDIVIDUAL'S RIGHT of publicity is a tort designed to address the unauthorized use of an individual's name or likeness for a commercial purpose. "Name or likeness" is interpreted broadly to include not only an individual's actual name, but also their stage name, pen name or pseudonym, as well as pictures, photographs, drawings, or other visual or audible representations of the individual. The right of publicity has been invoked successfully where the "likeness" was simply a sound-alike voice or a mannequin dressed and arranged with props that called to mind the stage persona of a famous individual.

Although the right of publicity may most often be thought of in connection with celebrities or other famous individuals, a person need not be famous to enjoy the right of publicity in many jurisdictions.

A "commercial purpose" is, generally, use of the individual's name or likeness to make money. Typical commercial uses include advertisements, displays of photos in store windows, testimonials, and the like. A use is not considered commercial, however, if the use of an individual's name or likeness is considered *newsworthy*—that is, if the defendant is actually using the individual's name or likeness in reporting the news. This newsworthiness standard does not, however, protect any use of a celebrity's image simply because the celebrity himself or herself is inherently newsworthy. The use of the name or likeness must be in conjunction with news reporting. Nor are publicity rights implicated if the use is editorial or artistic as opposed to promotional or merchandising.

Some states have also recognized another limited right of defendants to use an individual's name or likeness in advertising for their newspaper or magazine when that name or likeness is actually part of the content of the magazine or newspaper being advertised. This would not be true if the likeness were not part of the content, but was being appropriated solely to sell the publication.

The common law right of publicity has been augmented by statute in about half of the states. In many states, the right has been rendered inheritable so that it can be passed to surviving heirs or successors. Some states, like California, have searchable on-line registries which permit location of the party controlling the publicity rights of a deceased celebrity.

Because the right of publicity is a creation of state law, the law of the state where the person resides (or where he or she resided at the time of death) is usually the relevant law. Foreign laws may also come into play where the person is a resident of another country. Because each state or country's laws may vary in a number of ways, it is not possible to apply the same standards and guidelines to all uses.

The right of publicity has emerged as a very powerful and valuable economic right, particularly in today's society where celebrity status is its own commodity. Many famous people are able to trade on their fame alone, and therefore are likely to take action for any unauthorized commercial use of their name or likeness. Further, some businesses exist primarily to manage the publicity rights of living or deceased individuals, and these companies are also prepared to take action to protect those rights.

PRACTICAL POINTERS AND GUIDELINES

1) Keep in mind that right of publicity issues may arise with any individuals, not simply with movie stars, professional athletes, musicians, and other famous persons.
2) Even where use of a person's name and likeness is permitted as newsworthy, it is important not to create a false endorsement. Any single-issue, specialty magazine devoted to a particular celebrity should include a conspicuous disclaimer that the magazine is not endorsed by the celebrity (though this, in and of itself, will not eliminate exposure for a publicity claim). The title should make it clear that the magazine is *about* the celebrity and not endorsed or approved *by* the celebrity. In this regard, it would be helpful it the publisher's imprint is conspicuously placed above the title and/or the label "unofficial" or "unauthorized" were applied.
3) In cases where a celebrity is not the focus of a publication, but is tied to the subject matter due to his or her participation in a particular television program, movie, or other entertainment venue, use of the celebrity's image from that television show or movie may nonetheless impact the celebrity's publicity rights—even if permission is obtained from the owner of the copyright in the television show or movie to use images from that work.
4) Even when dealing with celebrities, focus on legitimately newsworthy information and avoid facts that are private in nature.

5) Remember that stock photos from an agency may bring with them right of publicity problems. Do not assume that just because you acquired a photo from a stock agency that there is no problem with the right of publicity. If you use a photo of Joe Montana on the cover of your sports management textbook, you are likely to have a problem.
6) When in doubt regarding whether the use of a particular name or likeness may constitute an infringement of the right of privacy, consult with your attorneys to minimize risk.

7) SPECIAL CONSIDERATIONS FOR ENDORSEMENTS AND TESTIMONIALS

ENDORSEMENTS ARE GOOD FOR BUSINESS. We know this intuitively. And a 2012 article in the *Journal of Advertising Research* confirms it empirically, reporting that in a study of more than 300 endorsement deals over nearly two decades, endorsements resulted in an average 4% increase in weekly sales of the endorsed products.

Sophisticated advertisers know this—Nike reportedly spends more than a quarter of its $1.7B annual advertising budget on endorsements—but so do unscrupulous advertisers. So the Federal Trade Commission has made it a practice to monitor and police the use of endorsements and testimonials and has, since 1980, published and periodically updated guidelines for their use. The basic principles are constant and straightforward:

- Endorsements must reflect the honest opinion or experience of the endorser;
- An endorsement may not convey to customers an express or implied claim that would be deceptive if made directly by the advertiser; and,
- Any connection between the endorser and the seller of the product that might affect the weight or credibility of the endorsement must be fully disclosed.

But the application of these principles has evolved and become more complex with changing methods and media of advertising. Let's take a look at how they are applied in several contemporary contexts.

READER ENDORSEMENTS

An ad on your website or copy on the back cover of your book that features readers touting what they have been able to accomplish with the aid of your book needs to be true, substantiated, and typical. The reader must have read and acted on the advice in your book. Any claims made by the reader will be evaluated as if you had made them directly and so you will need adequate substantiation to support the claim (including competent and reliable scientific evidence; reader testimonials themselves are anecdotal and do not constitute such evidence). The claims made by the reader must be typical of what other readers will achieve, you must have substantiation for this, and if you don't you must clearly and conspicuously disclose the generally expected result in the circumstances depicted. There was a time when the disclaimer "results not typical" was considered adequate for this purpose, but no more. The FTC now believes such disclaimers to be ineffective and so has amended its guidelines to require an express, affirmative disclosure of what is typical.

As an example, if the back cover copy of your new diet book featured before and after pictures of a reader with the claim that he lost 100 pounds in 100 days following the regimen prescribed in the book, unless this is typical of what other readers have experienced, your back cover copy would have to conspicuously disclose what the average reader does actually accomplish.

EXPERT ENDORSEMENTS

If your website or back cover copy includes endorsement by someone who would be perceived to be an expert (in the example above, this might be a medical doctor or nutritionist), then the endorser must in fact have those credentials and his/her claims must be based on an actual, professionally competent evaluation or test.

In the case of an expert, because this person is a professional in the business of providing expertise and advice for compensation, the FTC assumes that your readers will presume that the expert was paid by you. This represents a material connection that, were it not obvious, would have to be affirmatively disclosed since it would likely influence the credibility your readers assign to the endorsement. Such connections are not always obvious, however, as is sometimes the case with bloggers.

BLOGGERS

If a blogger buys your book and reviews it online, you are not responsible for what he/she says. But if you pay a blogger to review or plug your book or if you provide the blogger with free copies or with other perks with the understanding that he/she will promote your book, then there is under these circumstances a material connection between you and the blogger that will affect the credibility of the review in the eyes of consumers and this relationship must be clearly and conspicuously disclosed. There is no special language required as long as the consumer gets the information she needs to decide how much weight to give the review. It might be as simple as "Publisher A gave me a free copy of this book to preview and"

And, in the case of a compensated blogger, anything the blogger says will be attributed to you, so the blogger cannot say anything about the book that you couldn't say yourself. This means the blogger cannot make claims for which you do not already have in hand competent substantiation. If there is a failure to make a necessary disclosure, both you and the blogger will be responsible even if you did not exercise any control over what the blogger said. But the FTC has advised that when enforcement actions are necessary, it will be the advertiser, not the blogger, who is the focus of those enforcement actions.

REVIEWERS

The ubiquitous back cover blurbs have long been viewed with a skeptical eye. They are generally understood to have been culled and pared and isolated from context to leave just a few glowing superlatives. Consumers understand them for what they are and are not misled by them.

More problematic are the longer reviews left by reviewers presumed, but not always justifiably, to be independent. Amazon has purged thousands of suspect reviews from its website based on suspected connections or financial interests the reviewer might have in the book reviewed, with the author, with the publisher, or in a competing book.

DISCLOSURES AND DISCLAIMERS

When you are required to make a disclosure or disclaimer, it must be clear and conspicuous. This has always meant avoiding legalese and mouse type, but it takes on some additional complexity in the often pithy world of social media.

Proximity and placement of the disclosure are critical. The disclosure should be located proximate to the claim to which it relates and should be of equal prominence (comparable type size, weight, and color—if the claim is a flashing animation, then the disclaimer better flash, too). Readers should not have to scroll to find your disclosure, but if they do because the disclosure is lengthy or otherwise difficult to place next to the claim, then you must use proximate text or visual cues to encourage readers to scroll to the disclosure. A vague "see details below" will not suffice; but a more specific "see below for conditions on your right to return your purchase for refund" would likely pass muster. Where scrolling is necessary, then the disclosure should be unavoidable (i.e., the reader should not be able to proceed with a transaction without scrolling through the disclosure).

Hyperlinking to a disclosure is generally discouraged, especially when it comes to health and safety information. Do not simply hyperlink a single word, a short phrase in text, or a subtle icon. Instead, make your hyperlink obvious, label it to ensure that the reader understands both its relevance and importance, place it as close to the relevant claim as possible, and take readers directly to the disclosure.

Make sure that you account for viewing your promotional messages across all platforms (including small screen and mobile devices). A disclosure needs to be conspicuous regardless of the device on which it is displayed. Twitter, with its 140-character limitation, has its own special challenges. If your endorser is paid to tweet about your book, the endorser's tweets must disclose the connection. A hashtag like "#paid ad" uses only 8 characters and would probably be effective for this purpose. That the mode of social media will not reasonably accommodate a disclosure is no excuse. The FTC has taken the position that if any given method of reaching your audience cannot deliver the entire, non-deceptive message, then it shouldn't be used at all.

DIFFERENT RULES FOR THE INSIDE AND THE OUTSIDE

Until 2009, the FTC reviewed book advertisements under what it termed the "Mirror Image Doctrine"—i.e., ads that quoted or mirrored the contents of the book or that merely expressed the opinion of the author were thought to be shielded from government regulation by the First Amendment. But in 2009, after

SPECIAL CONSIDERATIONS FOR ENDORSEMENTS AND TESTIMONIALS 69

a series of court decisions tightening controls over commercial speech, the FTC abandoned its Mirror Image Doctrine. So now, while what is in your books is insulated from government editors by the free speech and press provisions of the First Amendment, the messages that appear on the back cover (or on your website or even on a blog influenced but not operated by you) to promote or sell your book constitute commercial speech, which enjoys only very narrow protection; and commercial speech that is deemed unfair or deceptive enjoys no protection at all. Just be sure you understand where the line is drawn between editorial and advertising...and the different rules that apply to each.

⑧ TRADEMARK PRIMER

If you are not a brand, you are a commodity.
—Philip Kotler, Professor of International Marketing,
Kellogg School of Management

A TRADEMARK IS A BRAND. TRADEMARKS ARE SHORTHAND signals used to signify that a particular product or service comes from or is endorsed by a particular company, association, or individual. Trademarks come in a number of different varieties—virtually anything that can serve to identify the source of goods or services and to distinguish that source from others can serve as a trademark. Brand names are perhaps the most common trademarks, but trademarks can also consist of logos, slogans, sounds, colors, a consistent "look" for a series of products, and the total image, appearance or even shape of a product or product packaging.

Trademark rights in the United States can arise simply by virtue of use of the mark in the stream of commerce. The formality of registration is not required to establish protected rights, although registration does provide added benefits. In other jurisdictions, however, trademark rights can arise from registration alone. Because trademark rights are territorial in nature, it is

Examples of different Types of Trademarks

Word Marks (including common terms, coined words, and names)	GENERAL ELECTRIC KODAK MCDONALD'S
Slogans and Phrases	DON'T LEAVE HOME WITHOUT IT CAN YOU HEAR ME NOW? JUST DO IT
Symbols and Logos	CBS Eye Penguin Books logo
Sounds	NBC Chimes Homer Simpson's "D'oh!"
Color	Owens Corning pink UPS brown
Trade Dress (including the look, shape or overall appearance of products and packaging)	*Time* magazine cover design (red border) Shape of the Coca-Cola bottle

Table 8.1

possible that a mark owner may have rights in one country but not in another. Publishers whose works cross national borders must therefore be sensitive to the various trade-mark rights that may apply wherever their material is published.

Trademark law plays two roles in publishing. It places constraints on how an author or publisher can use the mark of another. And in some cases, it can provide protection for series titles and character names.

LIMITATIONS ON USE OF THIRD-PARTY MARKS

Trademark law limits a publisher's ability to use or reference the trademarks of others. Once a party has established protected rights in a mark, any subsequent use of that mark or a similar mark that creates a likelihood of confusion in the minds of consumers as to source or endorsement constitutes infringement. Hence, using another company's trademark to identify your own publication, or copying or mimicking another company's slogan in a promotional campaign for your products, is likely to lead to a trademark infringement claim.

Famous marks—ones widely recognized by the consuming public—enjoy a slightly wider scope of protection. Where a truly famous mark is involved, any use by another party, whether likely to create confusion among consumers or not, may be precluded under the trademark principle of dilution.

There are, however, instances when it is permissible to use another company's mark. For example, it is generally permissible to use another party's mark to name that party's goods or services. Hence, you likely can use the KODAK mark in a headline of a feature that discusses Kodak cameras. This type of nominative fair use is permissible because it is difficult to identify a particular product or service without using its trademark. However, there are limits on the scope of nominative fair use. You cannot use more of the mark than is necessary to identify the product or service, and you cannot use the mark in such a way as to invite the reader to infer that the work is somehow endorsed or approved by the trademark owner. And when you use the mark of another, you should use it as a proper adjective and not as a noun (We are going to lease a Xerox brand copy machine. Not, we are going to lease a xeroxer.) There is no need to use the circle-R with the mark or to acknowledge the mark owner in a footnote (unless you have a contract with the mark owner that requires you to do this).

For example, a single-issue specialty magazine about the TV sitcom *Seinfeld* may be able to use the SEINFELD name in its title. Because the name alone is sufficient to identify the TV show, the principles of nominative fair use would not extend to allow the publisher to display the mark in the stylized script format associated with the show. Further, the SEINFELD name should not be displayed in a prominent fashion, should not be set apart from the remainder of the title, or should not be used in any other manner that would allow readers to assume that the publication was an official or licensed publication, unless the publisher has permission from Castle Rock Entertainment (the owners of the mark).

Other circumstances can also justify use of another's trademark as a fair use, including situations involving comparative advertising (which is essentially a variation on nominative fair use) and parody (which involves specific legal considerations beyond simply a judgment of whether a particular use is funny). Finally, keep in mind that the mere fact that a term has been adopted by someone as a trademark does not necessarily rob that term of its ordinary meaning or remove it from the lexicon. Hence, notwithstanding the fact that the Shell Oil Company owns the SHELL trademark, a publisher could still use the term SHELL in connection with a publication dedicated to collecting seashells.

Like trademark rights themselves, the available defenses to trademark infringement can vary from country to country. Hence, a use that may be considered fair (and therefore defensible) in the United States may constitute infringement abroad.

USING TRADEMARKS PROACTIVELY

Building a brand for your books is part marketing and part magic. Keeping competitors at a respectful distance from your brand is all trademark law.

In the book publishing context, a trademark is typically the name of a publishing house or one of its imprints, sometimes used together with a logo or slogan. These marks serve to distinguish the books published by that house from those published by any other—i.e., the trademarks serve as a distinctive indicator of source.

How do you select and protect a strong trademark? Two sometimes competing factors must be balanced to make a good trademark. The perfect trademark is at once both attractive and meaningful from a marketing sense and protectable from a legal sense.

DISTINCTIVENESS

The most important characteristic, which relates to both marketing appeal and legal protectability, is whether the mark is *distinctive*. That is, does it allow book buyers to distinguish your books from those of your competitor?

The more distinctive a mark, the broader the scope of protection. Distinctiveness falls along a spectrum like this:

Fanciful	Arbitrary	Suggestive	Descriptive	Generic
Always Protectable			May be Protectable	Never Protectable

Table 8.2

A *fanciful* mark is a made-up word or symbol with no ordinary English language meaning other than as a trademark. An example would be Anova Books, a British publisher of illustrated books.

An *arbitrary* mark has some known meaning, but that meaning has no connection to the goods or services with which it is used other than as a trademark. Examples include Penguin or Ten Speed Press.

A *suggestive* mark calls to mind a desired association between the word or symbol and the product or service in the customer's mind. Harlequin is a suggestive mark for romance novels.

Generic terms or symbols are never protectable for the same product or service. As a matter of fairness in competition, all providers of a product or service must be allowed to inform consum-ers of such basic information without restraint. "E-book" is now well established as the generic reference for digital books and could not now serve as a trademark for them.

Surnames, or family names, are usually not the best marks to choose. They often remain weak until secondary meaning has been established at considerable expense. Also, if the company is sold to an unrelated buyer or passed on to more than one heir, bitter and expensive legal battles may be fought unnecessarily over who has the right to use that surname as a trademark.

CHECKING AVAILABILITY

While most publishers think first of securing a registration for their mark, a thorough trademark search is probably more important than registration in the United States. This is because, under U.S. law, rights in a mark are based on first use, not registration. These are known as common law rights.

Clearing a mark involves considering three important factors:

(1) Protectability
(2) Availability
(3) Registrability

PROTECTABILITY

Protectability is a determination of what scope of protection, if any, is available for a chosen mark. Although you are free to call your house "Collector's Guide Press," you will not likely be successful in preventing other publishers of guide books from using "collector's guide" in their house name. Likewise, if you called your house "Computer Publishing," you would find yourself in a crowded field with nearly forty other live regis-trations for marks including the term "Computer" for use in connection with books. Such a weak mark is entitled to only a narrow scope of protection.

AVAILABILITY

"Availability" is a determination of whether you are or will be the first to use the chosen mark on or in association with your goods or services. This usually starts with a preliminary, or "knockout," search of the U.S. federal and state registers. How far the search continues will depend on individual circumstances. This is a critical issue on which you should consult a competent trademark attorney. You don't want to invest in building a reputation and goodwill for your brand only to discover down the road that an earlier adopter of a confusingly similar mark is in a position to force you to change it.

Searching will be more difficult and more expensive if your proposed mark is comprised of ordinary English language words for the simple reason that the search will be more likely to turn up more hits that require evaluation. Searches for proposed marks that are fanciful, because they are non-words, are more likely to come back clear. Of course, fanciful marks do not come packaged with the instant meaning and recognition that accompanies a suggestive mark, so they are less effective, at least initially, in communicating to your market. One compromise is to adopt a mark that, though not an English language word, is comprised of syllables from adjectives or nouns that convey features of or positive attributes about your books. "Microsoft" is a pretty good example of this.

REGISTRABILITY

Evaluation of a mark strictly for the purpose of registrability is limited to those marks registered or pending on the *Federal Trademark Register*. The U.S. Trademark Office does not search or consider state registrations, foreign registrations, or prior common law use during initial examination (though prior use by others may be raised in an opposition or cancellation proceeding).

The Trademark Office may refuse registration on the basis that the mark is generic, merely descriptive, primarily merely a surname, scandalous or immoral, or likely to be confused with another registered or pending mark. If the refusal is based on another pending application, your application may be "suspended" until the other application issues or is abandoned. This is one of the reasons why a thorough search must be as up-to-date as possible and include pending applications.

For a clearance search to be comprehensive and thorough, it should include a search for prior common law use of potentially conflicting marks. In many cases, your own knowledge of the industry is the best source. Also, trade journals, advertising media and news articles can be excellent sources for investigating common law use. Trademark lawyers typically use professional search companies to conduct these searches. Those companies maintain large, proprietary databases of business, product, and service names and logos.

REGISTRATION

Registration of your mark in the United States is not required; it is optional. Enforceable rights under state and federal laws are created by *use* of the mark, not by registration. There are many good reasons, however, for registering your mark. Registration offers the following advantages:

- Providing constructive notice of your claim to ownership of the mark.

- Allowing competitors conducting a clearance search to find your mark and avoid it.
- Providing a deterrent against infringement.
- Creating evidentiary presumptions that can be beneficial in litigation.
- Allowing use of the ® symbol.
- Establishing federal court jurisdiction.
- Creating a preference for Internet domain name registration.
- Allowing you to register with U.S. Customs to block counterfeit or infringing imports.
- Making available criminal penalties against counterfeiters.
- Conferring the benefits of incontestability after five years of continuous use, ownership and registration.

Federal registration requires use of the mark in interstate or international commerce. This usually requires a sale of books bearing the mark across state or international lines.

Registration is usually sought on the *Principal Register* if the mark is inherently distinctive or has acquired distinctiveness. If your mark is not inherently distinctive or you do not yet have sufficient evidence of acquired distinctiveness, you may be able to obtain registration on the *Supplemental Register*. Registration on the *Supplemental Register* and substantially exclusive use for five years may be adequate evidence of acquired distinctiveness and allow conversion to the *Principal Register*.

Most publishers readily recognize the value in their copyrights and publishing rights, certainly they are core assets in any publishing enterprise. It is less common for publishers to be so quick to recognize the value in their brand. It is, however, a substantial part of the difference between the value of your business as a going concern and its liquidation value. Give it the attention it merits and your efforts will be rewarded.

POLLYANNA, TITLES, AND TRADEMARKS

In the early 1900s, Eleanor Porter wrote for The Page Company of Boston the first of a series of inspiring books for children featuring a character named Pollyanna—a young girl who overcame childhood adversity and, through her infectious optimism, raised the spirits and aspirations of all around her. Each of the books in The Page Company's series incorporated "Pollyanna" in the title: *Pollyanna* and *Pollyanna Grows Up,* followed by a dozen others, and so the series came to be known as the Pollyanna series. Foreseeing commercial success for the series, The Page Company sought to stake out nationwide protection for Pollyanna by applying for a federal trademark registration for use of the word "Pollyanna" as the trademark for a series of books.

They were, ironically, overly optimistic. For whatever Pollyanna brought to the lives of the characters around her, she spelled nothing but trouble to protection for book titles.

The Page Company's application for registration was refused by the trademark examiner on the ground that "Pollyanna" was the name of a particular book and therefore merely descriptive of that particular book (use of the title being the only way by which the public could ask for it). According to the examiner, as it was the name of a product and not an identifier of the source of that product, Pollyanna was not capable of serving as a trademark.

In a later case concerning the issue of book titles as trademarks, a federal court explained that the title of

> a book is to the universe of published books as chicken soup is to food—simply a category and not a brand. Now that may make perfect sense if the title of the book is "Principles of Economics"—the first publisher to so title its textbook should not be able to preempt the field. It makes less sense for a book, and certainly a series, called Pollyanna.

Like it or not, this prejudice against trademark protection for single book titles has persisted, now for nearly a century, and is firmly ensconced in Trademark Office policy and practice. The formal position of the Office is simply that book titles must be refused registration—with one exception discussed below.

So we should just accept this broad brush treatment as an unfortunate fact of life and move on, right?

Not so fast, Pollyanna! Although you cannot obtain a federal trademark registration for your single book title, that doesn't mean you can skip the chapter on trademark law. There is yet a potential upside and also a significant downside.

THE UPSIDE

The one exception recognized by the Trademark Office is that the title of a series of books (as distinct from the title of a single book) can serve as a trademark. In order to understand why it matters whether trademark protection is available for titles (series or otherwise) you first need to appreciate what a trademark is and how it differs from a copyright.

Where books are concerned, a trademark can consist of any word, name, phrase, logo, symbol, or combination thereof that is used on the books to identify and distinguish a particular publisher's books from those of others or to indicate the source of the books. As an owner of trademark rights, the publisher has the right to prevent others from using marks that are identical or similar such that their use would create a likelihood of confusion in the relevant market as to source, affiliation, or endorsement. Through the use of a mark to distinguish its books, a publisher can keep its competitors at arm's length and prevent them from getting a free ride on its brands and its advertising.

But there is an important countervailing interest that constrains the protection we provide for trademarks—the right of the public (including competitors) to continue to use words in the English language in their ordinary English language sense. So generic terms cannot serve as trademarks—"book" can't be a trademark for books; and trademark protection for descriptive terms is sharply limited—this is the policy that causes mischief for book titles.

COPYRIGHTS DISTINGUISHED

But, you ask, doesn't copyright law provide protection for books? The answer is yes...and no. In contrast to trademark rights, a copyright is a set of ex-clusive rights in a work of original expression that vest at least initially in the author of that work. Here is one important distinction—copyright rights vest by default in the author; trademark rights vest in the party controlling use (this would commonly be the publisher).

Copyrights attach to works of original expression or authorship—the bar is low, but the Copyright Office and the courts have long maintained that titles and short phrases do not surmount it. So here is another important distinction—copyright law provides no protection for individual words or short phrases (and the copyrights in a book do not protect its title); trademark law does provide protection for words and phrases (provided they serve the source identifying function).

Included among the set of exclusive rights comprising copyrights are the exclusive right to copy the work and the exclusive right to prepare adaptations or derivatives. Copyright is not meant to protect against market confusion, only to keep others from conscripting the protected authorship. So a copyrighted work cannot be infringed except by someone who had access to the original because it is not just similarity that is precluded, it is similarity that results from copying. Here then is another important distinction—a copyright infringement claim requires proof of access and copying; trademark infringement is established through likelihood of confusion, irrespective of copying.

Finally, the term of copyright protection is measured by the life of the author plus 70 years—a very long time. Trademark protection lasts as long as the mark continues to be used in the stream of commerce as a source identifier—potentially forever.

SINGLE WORK VS. SERIES

So trademark rights have the potential at least to provide a different and additional layer of protection for publishers (and savvy authors) who are able to take advantage of this opportunity (as well as providing another asset for the publisher's intellectual property portfolio).

But given the Trademark Office's rule barring registration of single titles, where might this opportunity be found? The answer lies in imprints and series titles.

Publishers have long used imprints to distinguish and brand segments of their lists. Penguin's *Puffin Books* for children's literature; Random House's *Vintage Books* for trade paperbacks; or Simon & Schuster's *Pocket Books* for mass market paper-backs. An imprint is a source identifier for books of a particular description from a single source. The imprint is clearly distinct from the titles of the books published under the imprint and so does not suffer the trademark fate of individual book titles when it comes to registration of the publisher's rights.

Series titles are also registrable, as noted above. Where the series title is distinct from the titles of the books in the series, the process is analogous to that for imprints—Nancy Drew and The

Hardy Boys are two iconic examples (it appears, however, that Grosset & Dunlap failed to take advantage of "Nancy Drew" as a mark for its valuable series because its author team later bolted for Simon & Schuster with their series title in tow).

Sometimes, however, the series title is incorporated in the titles for the individual works. The "[fill-in-the-blank] for Dummies" series is a well-known example. Where this is the case, the Trademark Office has established three requirements. That portion which constitutes the claimed mark must:

1) create a separate commercial impression apart from rest of title – it has to be set apart and distinguished by, for example, size, type font, color, separation through the use of space or graphic elements;
2) be used on more than one work; and
3) be promoted or recognized as a mark for a series— mere use of the same words is insufficient; there must be evidence of promotion of the mark as a mark for the series or there must be evidence that purchasers or reviewers recognize the designation.

With respect to the second requirement, that the mark be used on more than one work, the Trademark Office has said that where the content does not change from one edition to the other, they will be viewed together as a single creative work. So none of the following variations/combinations would constitute a series:

- hardcover/softcover
- print/electronic
- unabridged/abridged

Nor would a single work that has been serialized or published in parts be considered a series (although periodical titles are registered, notwithstanding the fact that they are sometimes referred to as "serial" works, because the content changes from one issue to the next).

WHY GO TO THE TROUBLE AND EXPENSE?

It can cost up to a few thousand dollars and take from one to two years to clear and register a mark. Why go to all that trouble? For several reasons:

- Copyrights endure for a very long time, but trademarks are forever as long as they are continuously used and maintained.
- Copyrights vest initially and automatically in the author not the publisher and even when they are transferred to the publisher, the publisher's rights are subject to reversion (if the contract is breached by the publisher) and subject to a non-waivable statutory right of termination during a five-year window 35 years after the grant; trademark rights vest in the publisher (in the absence of a contrary agreement) and are not ordinarily subject to a reversion.
- Copyright infringement requires proof of copying; trademark infringement requires, instead, likelihood of confusion.
- A trademark registration carries with it a presumption of distinctiveness that after 5 years may become incontestable; without a registration, the plaintiff in an infringement action has the burden of proving distinctiveness.
- In cases where the publisher's non-compete rights, other contract rights, and copyrights are insufficient to keep its author from publishing elsewhere under his/her own name (read "Nancy Drew"), a trademark may permit the publisher nonetheless to maintain its titles as distinctive in the marketplace.

- And finally, a portfolio of trademark registrations adds to the publisher's intellectual property assets and can add value to its business and facilitate deals with lenders, investors, and purchasers.

THE DOWNSIDE

Even if you decide not to pursue development and registration of distinctive marks for your book series, you still cannot afford to ignore the subject of trademarks in connection with your list. Ironically, although a single book title is not capable of registration as a trademark, it can nonetheless be infringing of other marks—you may not be able to protect it, but you can be forced to stop using it.

In 1978, McGraw-Hill was enjoined from publishing a book that employed the trademark SCRABBLE in its title. In 1996, Simon & Schuster was able to successfully claim that William Bennet's *The Book of Virtues* had acquired secondary meaning so as to permit them to claim unfair competition under the Lanham Act to bar Dove from publishing a work under the title *The Children's Audio Book of Virtues*. Ty, Inc. has challenged the use of its trademark "Beanie Babies" in book titles. Likewise have the owners of the marks eBay, Cliff's Notes, Twin Peaks, and many others.

Notwithstanding broad First Amendment protection for literary works, including their titles, it is nonetheless unlawful for a publisher to make unauthorized use of another's mark in a title or on a book cover in a way that explicitly misleads or creates a strong likelihood of confusion about whether the mark owner has sponsored, approved, or endorsed the book or is affiliated with the book's publisher. While it might be acceptable to use the word "eBay" in the title of an unsanctioned guide to using the eBay brand on-line auction services (how else could the publisher let the reader know what the book is about?), it is not okay to use eBay's distinctive stylized form as the most prominent feature on the cover in a way that invites readers to infer that the book has been published or approved by eBay.

When in doubt, have your book titles searched and cleared before it is too late to change them. You don't want to find out, after 20,000 copies are sitting in the warehouse, that you have a problem with a title that appears on each cover, title page, and the running head of every recto page.

Pollyanna sold a lot of books, but don't be a Pollyanna when it comes to your titles and trademarks.

9) WHAT YOU NEED TO KNOW ABOUT USING THIRD-PARTY PHOTOS

IF YOU ARE USING THIRD-PARTY PHOTOS in a textbook or scholarly work there is some possibility that the use you contemplate may be defensible as a fair use—say your work is a text on photography and you are commenting on various techniques or styles, using portions of third-party images to make your point. Or, suppose your work is on a controversial political or social topic, as was the case in *Wojnarowicz v. American Family Association,* which involved the unauthorized photographic reproduction of fragments of 14 provocative works of art in a pamphlet critical of the public funding of such controversial works by the National Endowment for the Arts. While the artist quite naturally objected to this use of his works to attack the source of his funding, the political nature of the pamphlet, coupled with the fact that only a small portion of each original work was reproduced (ranging from 1 to 17 percent), convinced the court that the use was fair. But outside of use for a relatively narrow range of purposes (see Chapter 2 for a more detailed discussion of fair use), it is unlikely that your use will be excused as a fair use and so you will likely need permission.

And when it comes to photo permissions, there are just a few things you need to know.

OVER EXPOSURE

What the publisher did, according to the allegations in the litigation, was to play fast and loose with the photography it procured for use in its books. It would arrange with a photographer or stock agency for use of selected photos on the basis of knowingly underreported usage needs and on that basis get access to high-resolution copies of the photos at a price that was less than what it would have had to pay if it had made a full disclosure of the uses it planned. According to the complaints, the publisher would then put the high-res images into its own digital asset file, where it maintained them for future use, sometimes reporting the new or expanded use and paying additional fees later...and sometimes not at all.

The result of this chicanery was that this publisher was sued for copyright infringement in more than a dozen federal courts across the country, from Hawaii and Alaska to New York and Pennsylvania. The claims in these cases include allegations that the publisher's infringing conduct was pervasive and willful, raising the prospect of statutory damages awards of up to $150,000 for each image infringed...and across the cases there are thousands of images at issue. If the publisher lost these cases, it would have been exposed also for the attorneys' fees and costs of each of the many plaintiffs. What's more, the plaintiffs in some of these cases have also named the publisher's printers as additional defendants, and the publisher will likely have to bear the cost of defending and indemnifying all of them.

While you may not be so brazen about exceeding the limitations on your use of third-party photos as the publisher we describe above, today's business models for licensing third-party photography are sufficiently complex that it's worth taking a few minutes to review the basics and get familiar with the terminology.

CATEGORIES OF USE: EDITORIAL VS. COMMERCIAL

Professional photographers and stock agencies group their work into three broad categories based not on the nature of the photos but instead on the use to which they will be put: editorial, commercial, and retail. Retail use concerns photo-graphy commissioned for personal use, and thus is of little consequence to book publishers...except, perhaps, for that studio portrait supplied by your author for the back cover, a use for which the necessary rights have probably not been obtained. Editorial use concerns photography which will be used in a book, e-book, magazine, online, or in a presentation or video that is journalistic, educational, or expository in nature. Commercial use, conversely, concerns photography that will be used in advertising and promotion to sell or market a product (including a book), person (including an author), company (including a publisher), or service.

The distinction between editorial and commercial is particularly important because commercial uses typically carry a significantly higher price tag than editorial uses. And it is not always easy to draw the line between the two. While the use of a photo in the interior pages of a trade book is almost certainly editorial, the use of a photo on your web page may be editorial if it is associated with content being presented there; or it may be commercial if it is associated with a sales message. And if there is both editorial and promotional content on the same web page, it may not be easy to tell which predominates. Likewise, the photo used on the cover of your book is editorial, but a shot of the cover of your book (with the photo incorporated) appearing on an amazon web page offering your book for sale maybe be defined in your license as an un-included, secondary use that is commercial.

CATEGORIES OF ASSETS: ROYALTY FREE VS. RIGHTS MANAGED VS. COMMISSIONED WORK

"Royalty Free" and "Rights Managed" are terms that refer to the general scope of the license granted. First understand that Royalty Free doesn't mean free. Instead it is a term used to describe a license that provides for an up front, one-time payment in return for which you get relatively broad, non-exclusive usage rights. The obvious advantage to a Royalty Free image is that you pay a relatively small fee one time in return for the right to make multiple uses of the image. Be aware, however, that license terms vary from vendor to vendor and so even with a "Royalty Free" license there may sometimes be some sort of limit on the use that you can make of that image, either in terms of number of copies or in terms of length of time, or in terms of medium or purpose. The disadvantage to Royalty Free images is that the rights you get are non-exclusive and so the same image you select is also simultaneously available to others. Indeed, the others who also find it may have used some of the same search terms you used and so the odds that the same image will show up on the cover of a competing book or in an ad for a related product or service are better than you might think.

Commissioned work is the most expensive, because it is work staged or shot just for you and so the photographer's price to you will have to cover 100% of the value/cost of producing that work. You can pay this entire price up front in return for an assignment of the copyrights to the work. Or you can pay it one use at a time, for a series of exclusive licenses as your needs arise.

Rights Managed photos represent a compromise between

Royalty Free images and commissioned work. Rights Managed images are selectively licensed for a limited exclusive use, by market, by length of time, by geographic territory, by medium, and so on). The photographer or agency expects to spread the cost over several separate licenses over the life of the image and so the price is substantially less than comparable commissioned work at the same time that the likelihood of encountering a competing use of the same image is all but non-existent.

LIMITATIONS ON USE

So we have a spectrum of expense and associated rights from commissioned commercial work to Royalty Free work for editorial uses, but between the two ends of this spectrum the devil is in the details. The limitations on use can take a variety of forms from one vendor to the next. Here, then is a non-exhaustive list of the possible restrictions you may encounter.

- **Location/Placement** – like in real estate, location is important. Whether an image will be used on a book cover, on a chapter opener, in an internal illustration, or on a web page will have an impact on the price you are charged.
- **Size** – the size in which an image will be reproduced also often affects price. Size can be measured in terms of portion of a page (e.g., quarter page), or in inches (e.g., 5 x 4 inches), or in pixels (e.g., 2,000 x 3,500 pixels). Be sure that any size limitation encompasses the maximum size your use might require.
- **Medium** – the medium in which you will distribute your work makes a difference. Digital is more susceptible to unauthorized harvest and use than is print and photographers understand this and charge accordingly.
- **Quantity** – be sure that any quantity specified

comfortably covers at least your first print run (plus any allowable overage) and be equally sure to go back for license extensions *before* going to a second or subsequent printing.
- **Territory** – specifying world rights will certainly cover you, but you may end up paying for rights you don't exploit. Price the difference and make your decision accordingly. But don't forget to go back for an extension if an export opportunity becomes available.
- **Duration** – many licenses will be described as perpetual or unlimited in time, but Rights Managed licenses will have finite durations and even some Royalty Free licenses will have long but finite terms (e.g., seven or ten years or more) just to avoid open ended commitments. Watch for these and be sure to calendar them in a way that reminders are certain to pop up in sufficient time to get an extension or replace the image.
- **Versions** – if the license contains a limitation on versions, be sure that the limit encompasses the maximum number of design versions, editions, and any ancillary works in which the image will be used.
- **Language** – a photograph may be worth a thousand, language-neutral words, but look for limitations on language of the text used in the work in which the image will be incorporated and think not just about the book but also about the websites on which it may be featured.
- **Exclusivity** – there is rarely any confusion about the meaning of "non-exclusive," but "exclusive" can be defined by any number of metrics. Be sure to confirm that any exclusivity is clearly and unambiguously described. (And believe it or not, I

have seen the terms "quasi-exclusive" and "co-exclusive" each used in photo license agreements... I'm still wondering just exactly what they mean.)

The language used to express these limitations is critical. If you see a term that is unfamiliar to you, consult the Picture Licensing Universal System (PLUS) terminology glossary, developed by a coalition of associations representing photographers and other affected constituencies: *http://www.useplus.com/useplus/glossary.asp*. And when in doubt, add your own definition somewhere in the purchase documents.

WHERE TO FIND THESE LIMITATIONS

So now that you know to carefully examine any limitations on your license rights, where must you look to find these limitations? It would be terrific if there were one, universal place to go, but more often than not efficiencies of business communication have resulted in dispersion of the terms of the deal. They may appear in a pre-transaction document (in print or on-line form) that might be called a bid, a quote, an estimate, an assignment confirmation or the like. Although such a document, in and of itself, is merely an invitation to nego-tiate and not a binding contract, your acceptance of the offer, either by issuing a purchase order or simply making payment will have the effect of in-corporating the proposed terms, as well as any terms that might have been contained in any set of "Standard Terms" or "Terms and Conditions" attached to the offer document.

Sometimes there is a formal license document. This is especially likely if your transaction is effected on-line. In this event, in all likelihood you will be asked to click your assent as a part of completing your online purchase. Don't do this without closely examining the terms of that license that just flashed by.

Sometimes the terms appear in a post-transaction document, like a delivery memo, change order, or invoice. Although you can't be forced to accept these terms if they were not disclosed prior to your commitment, if you pay the invoice without examining it you will likely have assented to those after-the-fact restrictions.

CONSEQUENCES

What happens if, notwithstanding your best intentions, a restriction escapes your notice and your lapse is detected by the photographer or stock agency? Well, about the best you could expect is that you will be deemed in breach of your contractual commitment and held to account for what you should have paid for the uses you actually made. More likely, however, is a claim that you have made an unauthorized and infringing use of a copyrighted work outside the scope of any license you might have had. In this event, the copyright owner has some very potent strategic advantages and remedies at his/her disposal:

- **Actual damages** – they may elect to recover the profits you made from the unauthorized use of the profits they lost from your failure to take and pay for a license.
- **Statutory damages** – in lieu of actual damages, they may elect to ask the court for an award of statutory damages of up to $150,000 per work infringed in cases of willful infringement or up to $30,000 per work infringed where the infringement was not willful.
- **Attorneys' fees and costs** – on top of actual or statutory damages, they make ask the court to award reimbursement of their attorneys' fees and costs (this can be quite substantial – a lawyers' professional association reports that the national average cost to try a small copyright infringement case was $350,000).

- **Injunctive relief** – they may ask the court to order that you stop the infringing use and that you surrender all infringing inventory and reproductive materials for destruction.
- **Takedowns** – if your infringement is on-line, they may serve a takedown demand on your service provider, which will likely result in all or a portion of your website being disabled.
- **Indemnification obligations** – and since copyright infringement is a "no-fault" offense that reaches virtually every party who participates in the reproduction, distribution, adaptation, or public display of the infringing work, it is also likely that your printer and/or ISP will be named as additional defendants, increasing your cost and exposure.

It's said that you get what you pay for. When it comes to photography, that doesn't necessarily mean that low price equals low quality. Instead, a low price for a photograph probably means sharply limited rights. So look for a good price, but keep an eye out for the license terms and make certain they cover what you need lest you end up on the publisher end of a fight over photos.

10) SPECIAL CONSIDERATIONS FOR MUSIC

THE PRIMARY FORM OF INTELLECTUAL PROPERTY PROTECTION for music is copyright (though in the case of jingles, there may be trademark protection as well; see Chapter 8 for more on that subject).

In the case of a musical work, there are often two, separately protected embodiments: 1) the musical composition (the arrangement of notes and rhythms together with any associated lyrics) and 2) the sound recording of a performance of that musical composition. Each of these works is the product of separate authorship and they most often have separate owners. Typically, the copyrights in a musical composition end up owned by the music publisher (sometimes in shares with the composer/lyricist); the copyrights in the sound recording typically end up owned by the recording company.

USE OF SONG LYRICS IN TEXT

It is not uncommon for writers to incorporate a stanza or two of the lyrics from a well-known song to anchor a point or introduce a subject in an article or chapter in a book. Lyrics are, of course, subject to copyright protection and so unless your use qualifies as a fair use you need permission to reproduce them in a book or journal article. There are no bright-line tests for fair use of music, and the issue of whether or not the use of brief excerpts of song lyrics qualifies as a "fair use" is not often litigated. Music industry professionals will tell you that your use of as little as one line requires their permission. However, a couple of older cases decided under a now-superseded version of the copyright act suggest a different result.

In *Broadway Music v. F-R Publishing*, *The New Yorker* magazine quoted a portion of the chorus of a song in connection with its commentary on the death of silent film actress Pearl White. The court held that the use was permitted as a fair literary comment on Ms. White's death (she had appeared in a movie connected to the song). In *Karll v. Curtis Publishing*, the *Saturday Evening Post* reprinted eight lines of the chorus of the "official" song of the Green Bay Packers in a story about them. In both these cases, it was doubtless important that quoting lyrics without music would probably not have a negative impact on the commercial value of the songs themselves. The same analysis would likely obtain today under the current copyright statute.

With song lyrics, too, the strength of any fair use argument is bolstered if the amount taken is small and the use is closely connected to a legitimate comment on, or criticism of, the sentiment expressed in the lyrics (as opposed to appropriating song lyrics not for what they say about the mindset of the songwriter or the listening public but rather as a substitute for writing original verse).

OTHER USES OF MUSIC

The use of lyrics in text is not the only way you are likely to encounter rights issues in connection with music. Certainly this is the case if you are working in music theory or the performing arts. But in this age of interactive, multimedia education, it may also be the case in other disciplines as well.

HAPPY DAY...OR NOT

Mildred and Patty Hill were sisters living in Louisville, Kentucky, and teaching at the Louisville Training School for Kindergartners in the late 1800s. There, they collaborated to compose a collection of songs simple enough to be sung and remembered by kindergarten students. The objective, at least in part, was to expose their students early on to music with the expectation that this exposure would improve their students' language and math skills later on. This collection of simple songs was first published in 1893 under the title *Song Stories for Kindergarten* and included a piece titled "Good Morning to All." The song, by this title, is probably unfamiliar to you and it is firmly in the public domain having been first published long before 1923.

However, over the years since it was first published, Patty and Mildred altered the lyrics to help students celebrate an important annual event in their lives. This new version of the song, sung to the same rhythm and melody, you might recognize... as "Happy Birthday." The song, with these new lyrics, was not first published until 1935 and so, under the law in effect at the time, the updated lyrics, at least, would still be under copyright protection until the year 2030. The copyrights to this version have long been claimed by a unit of music publisher Warner Chappell and, indeed, it has reportedly generated more license revenue over its long life, at the rate of about $2 million per year, than any other piece of popular music. Every time the song was included in a movie or on television, every time the wait staff sang the song to a restaurant patron,

> every time it was performed in a concert hall or stadium, a license fee was charged; that is, until 2016 when litigation challenging, not the copyright status but, the legal sufficiency of Warner Chappell's chain of title was settled with the music publisher conceding that its chain of title was deficient and agreeing to a multimillion dollar refund of rights fees previously collected.
>
> Pete Seeger's version of "We Shall Overcome" and Woody Guthrie's version of "This Land is Your Land" have each been similarly successfully challenged in recent years, so that music publishers may be a bit less willing to press some claims in litigation going forward.

If you are creating a multimedia work and intend to perform and record your own rendition of a musical work for incorporation therein, you will have to clear rights from the publisher. If you propose to use, incorporate, or digitally distribute an existing recording, you will have to clear the necessary rights from both the publisher and the recording company. License terminology employed in the music industry can seem, to those not in the business, as somewhat arcane. Here is a list of the types of licenses you might reasonably need, the uses they cover, and the parties from whom you will probably have to get them:

- Music Publisher
    - *Mechanical license*—this license grants the right to perform and record a musical composition and distribute it to the public in physical form—e.g., music CDs, cassette tapes, LPs, and the like. It is the subject of a compulsory license in the U.S. That is, once the owner of the copyrights in a musical composition has released it in recorded form, anyone else can perform and record (or "cover") that song

and distribute physical copies subject to a duty to pay a royalty to the copyright owner at a relatively low rate set by law. Although the rate is set by law, compliance with the statutory formalities is somewhat burdensome, so many licensee elect instead to go through the Harry Fox Agency, an arm of the National Music Publishers Association that serves as a clearing house for managing mechanical licenses for its members.
- *Synchronization license*—if your performance will be recorded in timed relation to a motion picture or moving images, you will need what is called a synchronization license. There is no set rate or clearing house for these licenses and you will have to go publisher-to-publisher to negotiate them. Historically, the synchronization (or "synch") license only includes the right to exhibit the synchronized work theatrically or by broadcast. If you also want to distribute physical copies of the synchronized work (e.g., DVDs) you will also need a mechanical license (or will need to add what are called videogram provisions to the traditional synch license).
- *Public performance license*—this license pertains only to the musical composition, not to any associated sound recording, and is necessary if you plan to make a work incorporating the composition available by streaming, download, broadcast, or other performance. In the US, these rights are administered by one of three performance rights societies: ASCAP, BMI, and SESAC. Each of these societies manages its own portfolio of works and collectively, they manage virtually all of the existing body of music. If you want to know that you are licensed for public performance of any music that might be incorporated in your instructional or scholarly project, you will need

licenses from all three. They are heavily regulated, because of their concentrated market power, and so there is little negotiation as to price and terms for their licenses. They do, however, offer a variety of types of license for anything from blanket use of their portfolio to a one-time, special circumstances event. When is a performance public? More often than you might think. To perform a work publicly is to perform it at a place open to the public or at any place where a substantial number of persons outside of a normal circle of a family and its social acquaintances is gathered (including where the performance is broadcast or distributed to such a group in one place or in separate places at the same time or at different times). In other words, if you are doing it someplace other than your living room, it is probably a public performance. A performance open only to students enrolled in a class is a "public" performance for these purposes.
  - *Parody license*—this license allows you to alter a work in a way that is other than faithful to the original. (Recall that the right to make works derivative of a copyrighted original is one of the monopoly rights held by the copyright owner. So any material alteration in a copyright work requires permission unless it qualifies as a fair use.) Although this title is a bit of a misnomer, since true parody is generally protected as a fair use, it is nonetheless the terminology used in the industry to refer to unprotected alteration.
- **Record label**
  - *Master recording license (or master use license)* – if you plan to incorporate in your work an existing recording of a song (as opposed to recording your own performance) you will need a master recording license from the record label. There is no clearing

house for these licenses. You will have to go label-to-label for them. Unlike music publishers, whose primary business is licensing the exploitation of the musical compositions they own, record labels' primary business is producing and distributing recordings. Consequently, it will be harder to get their attention to your licensing request.
- *Digital transmission license*—while there is no public performance right associated with the sound recording, there is a digital transmission right. So if you will be using a sound recording in a work that you plan to make available via the internet, then you will need a digital transmission license. If your distribution is interactive, i.e., if users can select what they want to hear or when they want to hear it, then you will need to obtain this license directly from the record label. If, on the other hand, your distribution is non-interactive (think webcast or internet radio) then you can go to a clearing house, soundexchange.com, for a relatively inexpensive compulsory license.
- Artist/Composer
  - *Publicity license*—If you propose to use music in a promotional or marketing context, you may also need to clear publicity rights from any artists closely associated with the composition or the recording. See Chapter 6 for more about publicity rights.

PRACTICAL POINTERS AND GUIDELINES

1) If you want to incorporate music (as opposed to just lyrics) in your published multimedia work, you will need performance licenses. And if you have not pre-cleared the music selections, you will likely need performance licenses from all three societies.

Sometimes a host platform or publisher will have procured these licenses, but as often as not they will push the responsibility to you.

2) If you want to incorporate music in a presentation, you will need a license for this—the type(s) of license(s) you will need depend upon what you are using and what you are doing with it.

3) If you want to incorporate music in a video, you will need a synchronization license from the music publisher (if you are recording or incorporating your own performance of that musical composition). If you are using an existing recording, you will also need a master recording license from the recording company. The standard synchronization license covers only broadcast and theatrical performance. If you want to distribute the video as DVD copies or in some other tangible form, you will need a special form of sync license.

4) If you want to use the music in an advertising or promotional video, then in addition to the licenses noted above, you may also need publicity releases from any artists closely associated with the works.

5 If you plan to make the video available for download or streaming, see a lawyer. The licensing for this can be quite complicated.

6) Watch out for music popping up in places where you did not plan for it... user generated content, social media pages, contests, etc. You will be responsible if the site, contest, or event is operated under your imprimatur.

7) There are some exceptions to the monopoly rights of the copyright holders (including, notably, the fair use right), but they are just that—exceptions.

(11) SPECIAL CONSIDERATIONS FOR ART

"An essential element of any art is risk."
—Francis Ford Coppola

FRANCIS FORD COPPOLA WAS TALKING, of course, about aesthetic risk, not about legal risk. But when it comes to the currently pervasive attitude among art professionals about the use of third-party art in educational and scholarly publishing, he might just as well have been talking about legal risk.

In 2012, the College Art Association commissioned a study of practices and attitudes among visual arts practitioners regarding copyright and fair use. What they found was that the field had been overtaken by what they called a "permissions culture." Their report goes on to say that the process of finding illustrations for academic research was made more onerous by the conservative, risk-averse nature of the discipline, which shies away from invoking fair use even in instances where it is clearly applicable. About the unwarranted dependence on permissions, the CAA report opines that fair use is accessible, favored in the courts, appropriate for many uses in the field, and yet vastly underused, with serious consequences for the future of the field. In the survey conducted for CAA only one of nearly 3,000 respondents actually experienced a formal legal conflict as a result of using third-party art without permission.

Not only is fair use underutilized, but there are also other constraints at work—other tactics employed by art owners to extend their monopoly control over the art in their collections beyond the limits of copyright. Custodial institutions often charge fees for access to images, including those whose copyright term has expired. Variously termed access fees, permissions fees, and reproduction fees, they are in essence a service charge, though they are routinely mistaken as copyright permissions fees. In other cases, the custodial institution may condition access to public domain works of art, requiring that any third-party use be limited to reproductions of the art taken by the institution's own photographers so that although the underlying work is in the public domain, the image released to the public is a photographic reproduction subject to an independent claim of copyright (the latter strategy having been tested and rejected by a New York court in *Bridgeman Art Library v. Corel Corp* in 1998).

In response to the study results, CAA has published a set of best practices for fair use of visual arts: *http://www.college-art.org/pdf/fair-use/best-practices-fair-use-visual-arts.pdf*. When you are writing educational or scholarly pieces about artists, artworks, or artistic movements; or analyzing art within larger cultural, political, and theoretical contexts, these guidelines suggest that your use may qualify as a fair use if the following questions can be answered affirmatively:

- Is your use of the work, whether in part or in whole, justified by the analytic objective, and are you able to articulate that justification?
- Does your analytic objective predominate over that of merely representing the work or works used?
- Are the size and resolution of the published reproduction greater than is necessary for the analytic objective?
- In connection with digital-format reproductions of born-digital works, where there is a heightened risk

that reproductions may function as substitutes for the originals, have you been especially careful to articulate a justification for the use and the size and resolution of the reproduction?
- Does your reproduction represent the original work as accurately as can be achieved under the circumstances?
- Have you provided attribution of the original work as is customary in the field, to the extent possible?

I think it's fair to say that CAA believes that the research, literature, and teaching in the field would all be enhanced by a movement away from the permissions culture and toward a more effective and efficient reliance upon fair use where that is warranted. In scholarly writing for example, the authors of the CAA report suggest that at least some professors tend to steer their graduate students away from the study of modern and contemporary art and toward the nineteenth and earlier centuries because only access fees are involved with the latter and the former are likely to be just too expensive to publish adequately.

But if your institution or your publisher does not buy in to this enlightened philosophy, you will have to seek permission. And if you are not writing about art, but are merely using art to add color or interest to the subject you are writing about, then it is much less likely that your use will qualify as a fair use and you will have to seek permission.

This can be expensive. Costs for art permissions can average around $500 per image (some lower; and some much higher). So the permissions cost for a scholarly article might range up to a few thousand dollars. The cost for a major twentieth century survey, with several hundred images might easily exceed $100,000.

12) FINDING THE COPYRIGHT OWNER

WE'VE ALL BEEN THERE. You have the perfect photo, verse, song lyrics, vignette, to open your article, your book (or a chapter within it). Having labored long and hard to locate just the thing, you are now certain that nothing else will do. There's only one problem. It's not yours and either you can't determine who owns the rights, or you can't figure out how to reach them, or they're dead or out of business, or they won't answer you.

What to do?

Should you forge blindly ahead and risk challenge or suit on the one hand, or abandon your heart's desire on the other? Or is there a more elegant solution?

Well, if the answer were yes to the first question and no to the second, this would be the end of this chapter. But first understand that you only need permission to excerpt from works that are still under copyright protection, and even then where what you wish to use and how you wish to use it are not defensible as a fair use (See Chapter 2 for more about fair use). Assuming that you have answered these threshold questions and that seeking permission appears to be advisable, the obstacles that may get in your way are several.

THE PROBLEM OF ORPHAN WORKS

Copyright protection lasts for a very long time under current US law—for the life of the author *plus 70 years after the author's death* (or 95-120 years for works made for hire). And although we have a national public registry for copyright claims, its use is elective and not mandatory. So, copyright protection for a work continues long after the original copyright owner has died (or if the owner is a company, perhaps long after it has been dissolved or acquired). For these older, but still protected, works we still need licenses for certain uses, yet the owner may be much harder if not impossible to find. We call these "orphan" works and the problem they pose— that there is a substantial body of orphaned work that is effectively kept out of productive use because of the risk, however small, of a copyright infringement suit— has long been recognized but not yet resolved.

THE COPYRIGHT OFFICE STEPS UP AND CONGRESS STEPS OUT

In 2005, the Copyright Office undertook a study of the orphan works problem and a year later issued a 200-page report of its findings. In short, the Office concluded that the problem was real, was elusive to quantify, and required a legislative solution.

Two years later, in 2008, legislation was introduced in the 110th Congress that would have sharply reduced the damages available for infringement of an orphan work, provided that the user had done a reasonably diligent search to find the copyright owner (in compliance with search best practices that were to be established by the Register of Copyrights) and provided further that the user had included with the use an attribution to the owner where the owner could be identified. Unfortunately, this legislation on which so many years of study and effort had been spent died a quiet death, mired behind the bailout legislation that that so preoccupied the country and the Congress during that era.

The Copyright Office is looking anew at the problem in 2015 and issued another lengthy report, but any solution to the problem that might come from this effort is likely years away.

THE PRIVATE SOLUTION STYMIED

Meanwhile, in 2004 Google had undertaken a mass digitization project, reaching agreements with five major university and public libraries to scan the contents of upwards of 15 million books from these libraries' collections for the purpose of making this entire body of work digitally searchable. Google scanned these books without regard to whether or not they were still under copyright protection and without securing permission from the copyright owners of those books that were.

As a consequence, Google was promptly challenged in two suits, one initiated by several publishers and the other by a group of authors acting on behalf of a class of all similarly situated authors. The two lawsuits resolved pretty quickly into a protracted settlement negotiation that, had the settlement been approved by the federal court overseeing the two cases, would have resulted in a de facto scheme for dealing with a good share of the universe of book-form orphan works, albeit with Google alone at the controls. But the settlement was ultimately not approved and the litigation over this digital archive resulted, finally, in a finding of fair use in favor of Google (but without many of the use and permissions benefits that would have accompanied the settlement had it been approved).

But orphaned works are only part of the problem. There is also the problem of a work that is out-of-print, with a known publisher who won't answer or if it does answer disclaims responsibility. Or the artist who simply ignores your repeated inquiries. What can you do now to minimize your exposure whether or not the problem is an orphaned work, or a non-responsive owner or uncertainty about whether a work is still under protection or about who holds the rights?

PRACTICAL SOLUTIONS: BUILDING A RECORD OF DILIGENCE

Start by making and memorializing diligent efforts to track down the owner of the work you'd like to use. The specific steps that will be required of you depend upon the nature of that work. In general, you should consult the following sources.

The first place to start is typically the records of the US Copyright Office. For works registered or published since 1978, the records are available in an online database, searchable by, among other things, author, claimant, or title at *copyright.gov*. (The search program is not especially user-friendly, so while finding a direct hit will give you some comfort, not getting a relevant result does not necessarily mean that it isn't there, only that you didn't find it.) For older works, you will have to go to the Copyright Public Records Reading Room in Washington, DC to check the Copyright Card Catalog (or pay the Copyright Office or a private search company to do it for you). For more about determining the copyright status of any particular work, see Circular 22 "How to Investigate the Copyright Status of a Work," available at *copyright.gov*.

Your next stop might be published indexes of published material relevant for the publication type and subject matter—Books in Print (*www.booksinprint.com*), for example, or the Periodical Index (*http://pio.chadwyck.co.uk/marketing.do*), or any number of research tools available from ProQuest (*www.proquest.com*), or the Copyright Clearance Center (*www.copyright.com*). University and large public libraries may have their own indexes and catalogs of library holdings and collections that can provide information about the author or publisher of the work at issue.

If you have identified the original publisher of the work you wish to use but cannot locate them now, it may be because they were acquired or merged or dissolved and their assets dispersed. Consider checking sources that identify changes in ownership of publishing houses and publications, including Literary Market Place for book publishers (*www.literarymarketplace.com*), the list of imprints available from the International Association of Scientific, Technical & Medical Publishers for scholarly journals (*www.stm-assoc.org*), or for relevant country reprographic rights organizations (like Kopinor in Norway, see a list at *www.ifrro.org*) for published works in general.

If you have identified the author or creator of the work but cannot locate them currently, try biographical resources for authors like the Gale Literary Index (*www.galenet.com*), or business or personal directories or social media platforms (like LinkedIn or Facebook) or a search service like *www.pipl.com*.

Consider searching for other citations to the same work in recent relevant literature to determine if the citation to the underlying work has been updated by other users or authors.

Non-text media present special challenges. If what you have is a photograph or a video or a sound recording, there may not be an unambiguous title to search on…or an identified creator or owner. Although if what you have is a digital file, you may find some of this information in the metadata. But if what you have is just a photo print or a 70mm IMAX HD film or an audio cassette, determining what to search for is half the battle. Fortunately, digital search technology is helping to solve this problem. If you have an image, but you don't know where it came from you can actually load the image itself into a search engine on Google images to search for other instances of that photo on the internet, some of which may have author/owner information associated (*images.google.com*). Also in development is the PLUS Registry (Picture Licensing Universal System) at *www.plusregistry.org*.

For fine art, try Art Resource (*www.artres.com*), the Artists Rights Society (*www.arsny.com*), and the Visual Artists Rights Gallery (*www.vaga.org*).

For music, the searchable licensing databases at ASCAP and BMI can help you locate the artist, music publisher, and record label for any given work. If you have a physical copy of the recording, the liner notes should tell you who the composer and lyricist were, who the music publisher is, and with which PRO (ASCAP, BMI, or SESAC) the song is registered. The packaging should tell you who the record label is. Printed sheet music should also identify the composer, lyricist, and music publisher. And a digital copy may include music metadata.

MEMORIALIZING YOUR EFFORTS TO GET CONSENT

Keep a log of every step you took and source you consulted, unsuccessful as well as successful, to track down the authorship or ownership or copyright status of the work at issue. If you have identified and located an author or owner, and have attempted to contact them, keep a record of the date and substance of each of your requests for permission and every follow up attempt. If you receive no response from the rights holder, you may choose to accept the business risk of reproducing material without permission (and your publisher or academic institution may also relax its requirement that you obtain permission under these circumstances). In that case, a log of the attempts to contact the copyright holder will show a good faith effort to obtain permission. This, by itself, will not absolve you of liability—you cannot shift the responsibility or burden to the copyright owner by telling her that you will use her work unless you hear otherwise from her—but a record of respectful requests and diligent follow up coupled with a lack of any response can serve to reduce the size of any likely judgment and make the claim easier to settle as explained below.

SOMETIMES CONSENT IS PROVIDED IN ADVANCE

Scientific Technical and Medical Publishers and Social Sciences and Humanities Publishers have combined to establish a set of permissions guidelines with usage limits that pre-authorize certain uses without charge (*www.stm-assoc.org/permisions-guidelines/*). The Copyright Clearance Center in the US has an online licensing service that will allow you to request permission for use of material from millions of books, journals, magazines, newspapers and other works from thousands of publishers.

ACCEPTABLE BUSINESS RISK AND RESERVING FOR AFTER-THE-FACT PERMISSIONS

Sometimes the cost of clearing rights exceeds the likely cost of dealing with a claim after the fact. Recognize that you will not be in a great bargaining position and that the cost will almost certainly be higher than if you had been able to negotiate a license fee when non-use was still an option. However, if you make a reasonable estimate of what permission for similar uses would likely cost and if you set that amount aside in a reserve account for contingency claims, you won't be surprised. Your estimate in any given instance may turn out to be high or low, but overall you will have mitigated the consequence of later surfacing claims and will have a fund from which to satisfy them. And, there is a three-year statute of limitations for copyright infringement claims so at some point down the road your risk will have dissipated and you may be able to shift those reserves over into owner's equity.

WHY A MEMORIALIZED RECORD OF GOOD FAITH MATTERS

There are few absolutes or bright lines when it comes to copyright matters. So much is left to the judgment of the court or jury in a copyright infringement case, the boundaries so amorphous, the tests so subjective, that ensuring that you are more sympathetic than the plaintiff can go a long way toward moving the case one way or another. The threshold question of the copyrightability of plaintiff's work, the credibility assigned to any given copyright registration, the application of the four-factor test for fair use, the connection between profits and infringing conduct (and the proper allocation of same), the amount of statutory damages within the statutory range, the award of attorney's fees (and how much of them, if any) to a successful plaintiff, and (going the other way) the potential for an award of fees to a successful defendant if the claims prove to have been objectively unreasonable—none of these questions lend themselves to objective measure and confidence. And opposing counsel know this. Put yourself in a favorable light vis a vis the plaintiff and you make your case that much easier to settle.

INSURANCE AGAINST THE WORST CASE

For those risks you cannot reserve against and for the peace of mind that lets you sleep at night, consider purchasing media perils insurance coverage. Axis Pro is one source of such coverage: *www.axiscapital.com/en-us/insurance/us/professional-lines/axis-pro/multimedia*.

When typographers talk about orphans, they are generally referring disapprovingly to the solitary lines of type left at the bottom of a page when there isn't room for more from the same paragraph. Correspondingly, a widow is the term for a solitary line at the top of a page...and there is a mnemonic for keeping the two of them straight, "Orphans are left behind and a widow must go on alone." Don't be a widow when it comes to orphan works. Until we have a legislative solution, use the tools available to track down the authors and owners; record your efforts to find them and secure consent; and, for those cases where your efforts are unavailing but your editorial and business judgment tell you that the benefit from use outweighs the risk, reserve and insure for the occasional claim that might arise.

13 CONTRACTS AND THE ALLOCATION OF RESPONSIBILITY FOR PERMISSIONS MATTERS

IT IS LIKELY THAT THE PUBLISHER'S FORM CONTRACT will contain language that pushes complete responsibility for clearing permissions onto the author, but at the same time leaves final authority for what constitutes a sufficient license with the publisher. Language like this would not be unusual:

***Third-Party Permissions.** The Author shall clearly identify to the Publisher all materials for the Work and related materials that were not created by the Author, or are otherwise subject to legal rights of others. The Author shall be solely responsible for obtaining, at the Author's expense, permissions, releases, and other necessary authorizations, in form satisfactory to the Publisher, for the use of such materials in the Work and related materials in all media and all languages throughout the world.*

But this allocation of responsibility/authority is not especially fair or efficient. The author probably knows much less about clearing rights than does the publisher and probably has not previously dealt with any of the sources from whom permission might be necessary. Conversely, the publisher doubtless has some staffers who deal with permissions regularly and who have already established relationships with many commonly used sources, like stock photo houses and trade magazine publishers. Most established textbook publishers recognize this fact of life and will, if pressed, agree to handle the job of clearing permissions. Such a provision might look like this:

> ***Third-Party Permissions.*** *The Author shall clearly identify to the Publisher all materials for the Work and related materials that were not created by the Author, or are otherwise subject to legal rights of others. The Publisher shall be solely responsible for obtaining, at the Author's expense (the cost in each instance being subject to the Author's prior approval), permissions, releases, and other necessary authorizations, in form satisfactory to the Publisher, for the use of such materials in the Work and related materials in all media and all languages throughout the world.*

They may also agree to cover some, or occasionally all, of the cost… or at least to advance the rights payments and recover them out of royalties. Such a provision might look like this:

> ***Third-Party Permissions.*** *The Author shall clearly identify to the Publisher all materials for the Work and related materials that were not created by the Author, or are otherwise subject to legal rights of others. The Publisher shall be solely responsible for obtaining, at the Publisher's expense, permissions, releases, and other necessary authorizations, in form satisfactory to the Publisher, for the use of such materials in the Work and related materials in all media and all languages throughout the world.*

More difficult, but still worth trying, is to get them to agree to take and pay for less than rights in all languages and all media throughout the world, the latter being more convenient for them but rarely necessary for most textbooks.

In instances where the author will ultimately be called upon to cover the final cost of permissions, up front or out of royalties, it is important for the author to retain a final veto power once the cost of any third-party piece is established against the possibility that it isn't worth what it will cost.

YOUR REPRESENTATIONS AND WARRANTIES

The publishing contract, whether it's a book contract or a journal contract, will also include language requiring you to make certain promises about the manuscript submitted for publication—that it's an original work, that it doesn't infringe the intellectual property rights of any third party, that it isn't libelous, and so on. Such a commitment from the author is both appropriate and absolutely necessary because only the author is in a position to know whether the things promised are true—there is no database a publisher can search, no amount of diligent, independent, research it can do that will disclose for certain whether the author's work is original and claim-free. If you have not handled the rights clearance and permissions matters successfully, one or more of these representations and warranties will be breached and you will likely be responsible for dealing with the consequences.

But although most publishing contracts have such provisions, with a certain core content common among them, in the course of my practice I have encountered many variations, some of which suggest that the risks to be addressed are not always well understood. Let's examine some of the common elements first, then some of the less typical variations, and finally the indemnity language that puts the teeth in these provisions.

THE INTRODUCTION

The Author represents and warrants to the Publisher that:
Lawyers say "represents *and* warrants" not to be redundant (though we are sometimes just that). Strictly speaking, a representation is a promise that the fact asserted *is* true at the time the contract is entered. A warranty, on the other hand, is a promise that the thing asserted *will be* true or *will happen* (or not happen, as the case may be) in the future. What typically follows this phrase in most publishing contracts is a mix of some

representations, some warranties, and some that are hard to categorize due to sloppy drafting. The distinction between them has the potential to be significant because the legal consequences that follow breach of a representation are different from those that follow breach of a warranty (rescission and restitution being available as remedies for the former but not for the latter).

THE MOST COMMON REPRESENTATIONS AND WARRANTIES

the Author is the sole and exclusive author of the Work and the sole and exclusive owner of the rights herein granted to the Publisher;

With few exceptions, the copyrights in a manuscript vest automatically in its human authors. Because registration and notice are not pre-requisites, there is no independent search or examination available that will reveal all of the potential claimants to a manuscript—the publisher is entirely at the mercy of its author with respect to disclosure of this information. There is no good reason for an author to refuse to make this representation because it is based on information that he/she necessarily has. If there is someone else with a claim to the manuscript, e.g., a ghost writer or undisclosed collaborator, the publisher will want to know that so that it has an opportunity to secure all of the exclusive rights to the work from every potential claimant or, if for some reason the publisher should choose not to do so, that it does that knowingly.

the Author has not previously assigned, pledged, or otherwise encumbered the Work;

Similarly, if the author has pledged rights in the manuscript as security for a loan or otherwise, the publisher wants to know that as well, lest it be later surprised by a party with a claim superior to its claim. Here, with respect to this particular risk, there are some steps that could be taken independently to ensure that the publisher's claims have priority, but they are somewhat cumbersome and not routinely undertaken by publishers.

the Work has not heretofore been published, except as follows: [describe]

If the work has been published before by another party, the publisher will want to do a search of the Copyright Office records to determine whether there is a public record owner of the copyrights in the previously published edition so that it can take any steps necessary to complete and update the public record chain of title.

the Work is not in the public domain;

While it is exceedingly unlikely that a publisher could be unknowingly enticed to publish a public domain work, if it were presented with a public domain work that it was for some reason interested in republishing, it could freely do so without the need to enter a contract or pay royalties to anyone. Again, there is no search the publisher can independently do that is guaranteed to identify every public domain work, but the genesis of any work is certainly known by the author who presents it.

the Work does not infringe any statutory copyright or common-law literary right of any third party;

Only the author knows for certain how the manuscript came to be created and no matter the diligence the publisher employs it cannot be certain, absent the author's disclosure, that third-party content was not incorporated. You will sometimes see, as in the language above, a reference to "common-law literary rights," which is a carryover from contracts written before 1978, when an overhaul of U.S. copyright law rendered all copyrights statutory and did away with the concept of common law rights equivalent to copyright (except for a very narrow category of sound recordings). The language is sometimes allowed to remain because it does no harm and because lawyers are reluctant to surrender any ground once gained.

the Work contains no matter which is scandalous, libelous, or defamatory, or which infringes any trade name or trademark, or which violates any right of privacy or any other proprietary right;

Although the publisher cannot necessarily spot every privacy violation or trade secret misappropriation without some input from the author, there are steps that can be taken (and should be taken for manuscripts on certain subjects) to identify unacceptable risks in these areas. This provision is routinely included in the contracts, not as a substitute for the publisher's exercise of appropriate diligence but to ensure that the author also has a direct and substantial stake in disclosing and dealing appropriately with these risks.

there are no errors or omissions in any recipe, formula, design, or instruction in the Work which might harm the user;

In the U.S., the First Amendment provides publishers with a great deal of freedom to publish what they see fit without fear of liability to dissatisfied readers. There have been a few noteworthy exceptions, however, where a publisher was held to be liable for egregious errors—e.g., incorrect airport approach coordinates that led to a fatal plane crash and faulty chemical experiment instructions that produced an explosion injuring a student. Presumably your bona fides, as author, include professed expertise on the subject at hand and so it is appropriate for you to be held accountable for any claim that might result from an error or omission, regardless of how unlikely. Apart from the liability, it's just bad business and worthy of an author's attention, which this representation may help to focus appropriately.

THE VARIATIONS

Less commonly encountered, but worthy of comment for one reason or another, are the following provisions, some of which are flawed in purpose and others of which are just poorly drafted:

all statements of fact contained in the Work are true or are based upon reasonable research;

This is one of the provisions that should provoke a raised eyebrow. Not every error of fact in a manuscript is of equal consequence and many of them have no potential to give rise to a third-party claim—to write, for example, that the U.S. is comprised of 51 states would be an error, but not one you could be sued for. No one wants to publish a manuscript with errors, but to include such a provision in the author's reps and warranties would be akin to requiring a warranty that there are no typos, misspellings, or errors of grammar and would dilute, by association, the more important issues worthy of focused attention.

the material in the work is verifiable as fact;

Likewise, only worse, is this language, which excludes all opinion (and doesn't, strictly speaking, exclude any errors as it only requires that the material be capable of verification, not that it be actually verified).

the Author has full power and authority to enter into this Agreement;

Here again, probably a case of overkill. Most authors enter publishing contracts on behalf of themselves individually, and if they happen to be underage or legally incompetent one would hope the telltale signs had not escaped the publisher's notice. This language is common in corporate acquisition documents where it matters that the entity that is party to the contract be empowered to do so and it may be that it was inserted once, for an author contracting in the name of his/her personal services corporation for tax reasons, and not subsequently removed.

the Author has no knowledge of any claims, actions, or proceedings, pending or threatened, against Author and affecting the Work, other than those disclosed to Publisher in this Agreement;

One would think that an author who was already being sued for libel by the subject of one book would disclose this in a pitch to another publisher for yet another book about the same notorious subject. That an author once neglected to do this accounts for the inclusion of this rep in at least one publisher's contracts.

the Author has not misrepresented the Author's academic or other credentials and will not provide any false or materially misleading documents concerning the work;

I can understand why this would be of potential concern, but like typos and spelling errors, not every concern merits attention in the author's reps and warranties. If the author has run afoul of this rep, there will doubtless be other grounds for rescinding or terminating the contract.

the work does not disclose any information given to the author on the understanding that it would not be published or disclosed;

Although this goes a little beyond trade secrets to reach information that is merely confidential and not necessarily also proprietary, I'm not sure that it covers anything not already addressed in the common core of author representations.

no material in the work plagiarizes any other work;

Plagiarism is not a synonym for copyright infringement and although disdained in academic circles it is not necessarily illegal. Plagiarism means to pass the work of another off as your own. You can plagiarize a public domain work, but you cannot infringe it. To the extent that plagiarism might produce a cognizable claim, it is already covered by the other representations and warranties and to the extent that it would not, it probably does not merit extra attention here.

Regardless of which of the foregoing representations and warranties you negotiate in your publishing contracts, savvy authors and agents will press to limit their application to the manuscript *as supplied by the author* and will want to expressly exclude any changes made or material added by or at the direction of the publisher. And if the publisher has agreed to take on responsibility for obtaining permissions, you should also exclude *third-party material identified by the author as such* so that you don't end up responsible for obtaining a permission that the publisher promised to get or for the publisher's failure to limit use of the material to constraints to which the publisher agreed.

More likely to draw resistance from a publisher is the co-author who resists the notion of "joint and several responsibility" and wants to disclaim responsibility for the contributions of his/her co-author. Though reasonable in concept, this allocation of responsibility can prove impossible to execute because of the difficulty of parsing the contributions of one from the other where their writing is truly collaborative. Even more likely to draw resistance is the author who wants to qualify any of the representations with a knowledge limitation—e.g., "to the best of the Author's knowledge…" or "the Author does not know or have reason to know…" Such a request will almost always be rejected out of hand.

THE TEETH: INDEMNIFICATION AND DEFENSE OBLIGATIONS

Most contracts will also require the author to indemnify the publisher for any damage or cost incurred as a result of any breach of the author's representations or warranties. Some contracts will also include within the author's responsibility any "alleged" breach, meaning that the author is responsible for defending all claims, without regard to whether they eventually prove to have merit. Knowledgeable authors/agents will object to this on the grounds that frivolous claims are a cost of doing business that should be borne solely by the publisher. There is, however, some distance between a claim that is simply frivolous and one that is just finally adjudged to be without merit.

The indemnification provision will also typically:

- Give control of the defense to the publisher
- Give the publisher authority to settle any claims (sometimes conditioned upon the author's reasonable consent)
- Allow the publisher to suspend royalty payments while any claim is pending
- Require the publisher to provide prompt written notice of any claim to the author
- Oblige the author to cooperate in the defense
- Provide that the indemnity survives termination of the contract
- Extend the indemnity obligation to also encompass claims against the publisher's licensees, assignees, and distributors

While there is room to negotiate on some of these provisions without materially compromising either party's bona fide interests, publishers are often leery of the possibility that material changes in this portion of the publishing contract may have an adverse impact on their media perils insurance coverage.

Authors and agents will sometimes ask that the author be added as an additional named insured to the publisher's media perils insurance policy. Although this request can be accommodated, in actual practice it provides little real comfort for authors as they are still responsible for a deductible or self-insured retention that is typically in the six-digit range. The better course for most authors (and less burdensome for the publisher) would be for the author to purchase an author's policy with a much smaller deductible. Axis Pro is one source of such coverage: *www.axiscapital.com/en-us/insurance/us/professional-lines/axis-pro/multimedia.*

14) DEPICTION RELEASES, PROPERTY RELEASES, LOCATION RELEASES, AND PERMITS

IF YOU ARE STAGING YOUR OWN STILL PHOTOGRAPHS for a book or journal article or if you are shooting video for a multimedia project and if your staging of the shoot will include identifiable humans or recognizable places, or if it requires access to property (private or public), then you may need, or want, to use a written release from the subject or from the property owner to eliminate, among other things, the potential for a privacy or trespass claim.

The release is, in essence, a legal contract wherein one party consents to participate in the subject activity and agrees to waive certain claims that party might otherwise be able to assert. The other party, also makes certain commitments, the nature of which varies from situation to situation.

In every state in the US, there are certain elements that are essential to the formation of a legally binding contract, or more specifically for our purposes here, a legally binding release. One of these elements is that each of the parties must have legal capacity. Among other things, this requires that they be of the age of majority (so releases from minors require approval of a parent or guardian). Another is that there be an agreement, comprised of an offer and an acceptance of that offer. Each side, in the exchange of offer and acceptance, must be supported by something called "consideration." Consideration, in this context means that the promises made by one party to the agreement have to be made in exchange for some promises from the other party—this could be a promise to do something that party is not otherwise obliged to do; or it could be a promise to refrain from doing something that party otherwise has a legal right to do.

In the case of a release, the releasing party is agreeing not to assert claims they might otherwise have. The party getting the release must make a concomitant commitment of some sort or something in return or there will be no consideration for the release. Sometimes this concomitant commitment is to make a token payment of $1 or $5 or $10. Sometimes the something in return is the opportunity for public exposure that comes with depiction in a published work or a publicly performed multmedia project. So you will see that the specimen release forms in the Templates section at the end of this book generally include a recital of some form of consideration to memorialize the fact that consideration was present and part of the bargain.

In some cases, the use of a release is a risk management strategy. In other cases, it is a necessary step. What goes into these releases and permits depends on which form of release it is, what you need to accomplish, and how much bargaining leverage you have.

DEPICTION RELEASES

When your photograph or video clip will include the image of a person who is recognizable, if there is a chance that person is in a place where he/she has a reasonable expectation of privacy then you may want a release from that person. And you may want to get releases from everyone who appears in your photos or videos as a matter of course if your publisher, broadcaster, internet host, or insurance carrier requires it as a part of their risk management strategy.

The depiction release will, of course, include a release of any potential privacy claim. But it will also likely include an affirmative right to crop or alter or edit the image, or to lay in an audio track in the case of a video recording. It may have the subject waiving any right to review or approve the resulting work. It will probably have the subject also releasing false light, libel, and publicity rights claims. It may waive any right to compensation, acknowledging at the same time some other form of consideration or reliance. And in some cases, it may obligate the subject to cooperate with the shoot, to provide access to relevant information or documents, and to refrain from cooperating with any potentially competing publisher or project.

PROPERTY AND LOCATION RELEASES

In the case of a property or location release, privacy claims may still be an issue but the primary focus is more likely to be access to the private property or real property of some other and the waiver of any trespassing claim that might otherwise be asserted. Private property might include access to a car or other vehicle or access to some other artifact (e.g., jewelry or a Heisman trophy). In the case of real property, the subject might be a house, an apartment, a business facility or a hotel. In a property or location release, the central issues (apart from the release itself and the supporting consideration) are likely to be the time and terms of access, an obligation to take reasonable care of the loaned property, and an obligation to return it at the end of the term in substantially the same condition in which it was provided.

THE LAW OF UNINTENDED CONSEQUENCES

In 2008 in Louisville, Kentucky, an office building was scheduled for demolition to make way for a new sports arena. The demolition was to be accomplished by implosion and so promised to be something of a public spectacle. A production company producing a series about spectacular demolition projects for a well-known cable channel wanted to take advantage of this event to record it for inclusion as a segment in one of its upcoming programs.

More out of habit than strategic planning, the production company presented the building owner with its standard location release. This implosion was only going to happen once, after all. There would be no re-takes. So the production company naturally wanted cooperation from the building owner so that the production company was in continuous communication as detonation time approached and had all of its people and equipment in place to capture the event.

All of this was memorialized in the location release. What they forgot was to strike that provision of the release that obliged them, when the shoot was concluded, to return the building to its owner in the same condition it was in when they obtained access. That, as they say, was not happenin'. The moral of the story is, a form agreement is a place to start. It is not often a one-size-fits-all solution and it is not a substitute for thoughtful evaluation.

PERMITS

If the location you have chosen for your shoot is not on private property, but is instead in a public space like a street, a courthouse, or a park, you will likely need a permit. These permits are managed and issued by the governmental entity in whose jurisdiction your chosen space is located. It might be a federal, state, county, or municipal body. Or it might be a park board.

Most commercial filming taking place within a public space will require at least one, and maybe several, permits—one from the governmental unit managing the property, one from the relevant division of labor if you are using minors, and others if your shoot will involve animals or pyrotechnics. There will generally be a fee for any required permits, to cover the administrative costs of issuing the permit and to cover the cost of any required supervision of the shoot.

The standards for video are a little more stringent than those for still photography. For video, you will likely need a permit for any commercial filming, meaning recording by any technology for an entity for a market audience with the intent of generating income. Still photography will likely require a permit only if the shoot will take place where or when members of the public are generally not allowed, when the shoot involves models, sets, or props not a part of the location's natural setting, or when the governmental body will incur additional costs to monitor the activity.

15) INSURANCE AND RESERVES FOR MANAGING RISK

SOMETIMES, TAKING A RISK with a difficult or impossible to get permission is a calculated business decision. But even if you are cautious about clearing rights and diligent about seeking permissions, mistakes happen. And even if you haven't overlooked anything, you may still get hit with a meritless claim. What's an author to do?

Well, there are at least a couple of strategies for managing the residual risk that accompanies any publishing endeavor, regardless of how careful you have been. One such strategy involves the use of insurance. The other involves anticipating and reserving for the settlement of any claims that might surface.

TYPES OF INSURANCE

Depending on the nature of the claim, there may be coverage or an obligation to defend under the "advertising injury" provision of your Comprehensive General Liability (CGL) policy—don't be misled by the description, this coverage is much broader than it sounds. Historically, advertising injury has been defined in CGL policies to include: libel, slander, invasion of privacy, copyright infringement, and misappropriation of advertising ideas. There are a couple of important limitations to the applicability of advertising injury coverage. First, it does not apply to intentional acts. So it will not address the risk that you face in going forward without permission in cases where you have reason to know that you need it. Second, it is intended to cover advertising and incidental publishing activities that a business undertakes to promote its goods and services and does not cover claims that arise directly from the conduct of your business if your primary business is publishing, advertising, broadcasting, or internet-based. But if your primary business is research or teaching and the publishing activity is incidental to that, you may have recourse.

Alternatively, there are more specialized policies that are specifically designed to cover businesses whose primary function is publishing, broadcasting, or internet-based. Included among these are policies sometimes called "media perils," sometimes "errors and omissions," sometimes "cyber-risk" or "cyber-liability" and sometimes "professional liability" policies. Even with these policies, coverage does not encompass activities that are knowingly infringing. These policies are instead intended to cover situations where a clearance claim arises even though the insured has taken all advisable clearance actions.

THE APPLICATION PROCESS

Obtaining a policy of media perils insurance starts with the completion of an application. You will be asked a series of questions about your business. The purpose of these questions is to provide the insurer with information it will use to evaluate your risk and determine the cost of your coverage. As a consequence, the coverage you get will be conditioned upon the veracity of your responses to the questions in the application and the completed application will be incorporated by reference into any contract of insurance that results.

Among the questions you may be asked are:
- Whether you have written agreements with all the people who have contributed content to your work.
- Whether you have obtained written releases from all recognizable people and distinctive locations depicted in your work.
- Whether you have appropriate licenses for all music, film clips, artwork, quotes, photography, and third-party material incorporated in your work;
- What has been your claims experience.
- What is the nature, frequency, and volume of your publication activity; and,
- Who is your publishing/media counsel, if you have one, and what is his or her experience.

Any policy you obtain will include coverage limits, per claim and per policy. And they will include a deductible or self-insured retention—the amount of the claim you must pay before the insurance coverage kicks in. High limits and low deductibles lead to high premiums. Conversely, low limits and high deductibles decrease coverage cost.

Most policies obligate the insurer to defend and indemnify the insured. But the duty to defend is broader than the duty to indemnify. So as long as there is a colorable claim, the insurer is obliged to undertake and pay for defense of that claim. The obligation to indemnify is only triggered if the claim is actually sustained. As a practical matter, however, most claims are settled with the participation of the insurer and with the insurer covering the cost of settlement up to the policy limits.

CLAIMS-MADE VS. OCCURRENCE-BASED POLICIES

Insurance policies can be issued on either a claims-made or an occurrence basis. Claims-made coverage extends to claims that arose during the policy term. So if a claim arises from a work first published in 2015, you would look to the policy in effect in 2015 even if the claim was not asserted until 2017. If you pub-lished one work in 2015, a one year policy covering the year 2015 would be sufficient to cover any claim arising as a result of that one published work.

Occurrence-based policies, conversely, cover claims asserted during the policy period. So if your policy is an occurrence-based policy, you must maintain coverage for at least the period of that statute of limitations for the types of liability you seek to address; e.g., three years for copyright infringement claims.

COST

Sam Ewing was a professional baseball player. But he knew about more than baseball. He said this about inflation: "Inflation is when you pay fifteen dollars for the ten-dollar haircut you used to get for five dollars when you had hair."

Anything we might say here about the cost of insurance is likely to be highly generalized and true for only a short time, in part as a consequence of that inflation thing Sam Ewing was complaining about. With that caveat, we can say that you should be able to find insurance policies of the type we describe with coverages ranging from $0.5 million to $40 million and at rates from $2,500 and up, depending on the size and nature of your publishing program and the deductible you are willing to absorb. (See the resources section at the end of this book.)

ACCEPTABLE BUSINESS RISK AND RESERVING FOR AFTER-THE-FACT PERMISSIONS

Sometimes the cost of clearing rights exceeds the likely cost of dealing with a claim after the fact. Recognize that you will not be in a great bargaining position and that the cost will almost certainly be higher than if you had been able to negotiate a license fee when non-use was still an option. However, if you make a reasonable estimate of what permission for similar uses would likely cost and if you set that amount aside in a reserve account for contingency claims, you won't be surprised. Your estimate in any given instance may turn out to be high or low, but overall you will have mitigated the consequence of later surfacing claims and will have a fund from which to satisfy them. And, there is a three-year statute of limitations for copyright infringement claims and one to three years for libel claims (depending upon the state whose law applies) so at some point down the road your risk will have dissipated and you may be able to shift those reserves over into owner's equity.

16) PERMISSIONS, RECORD KEEPING, AND DUE DILIGENCE

IN SOME SITUATIONS, PERMISSION IS PLAINLY REQUIRED to avoid infringing a third party's rights. One example would be the use of a third-party image for the cover of a book or to illustrate a journal article.

In other situations, asking for permission is the path of least resistance. Indeed, securing permission for the use of intellectual property owned by another—whether it be likeness rights under the right of publicity, rights to reproduce text under copyright law, or the right to use a company's trademark under trademark law—is often more cost effective than responding to a claim for intellectual property infringement, even when your use of the intellectual property can be defended, whether as fair use or otherwise.

Whenever you obtain permission, whether the request is informal and unwritten or in the form of a fully executed contract, you will in effect be taking on private, voluntary obligations governed by contract law. Therefore, consultation with legal counsel may be in order.

OBTAINING PERMISSIONS

Where permission is required or advisable, the first step is to determine who to contact for permission. Often it is the publisher or another third party, rather than the author, who holds the copyright (or a subset of exclusive rights under copyright governing the use you wish to make). Generally speaking, the relevant rights owner for books, scholarly journals, and consumer magazines will be the publisher; the rights owner for articles in trade or commercial journals is more likely to be the author; rights in photographs are often retained by the photographer (although if the photographs have been obtained through a stock house or from a PR person/agency, these rights have been cleared); the rights to music are held by a music publisher (for the musical composition) and a record label (for the sound recording); and rights in audiovisual works are often held by the production company. Note that sometimes a published work will itself contain excerpts from other works that are reproduced with permission. If you want to reproduce an excerpt that includes such materials, you must contact the original grantor of permission as well as the second publisher (or simply the original grantor, if all you wish to reproduce is the original grantor's work).

In the request, identify exactly what you wish to reproduce. Include copies of the original for easy reference if possible, not only the pages you wish to reproduce but also the title page for the work. In addition, describe as precisely as possible what you plan to do with the copyrighted material. If possible, include a draft of the work in which the material is proposed to be used.

When drafting permission requests, think broadly in terms of all of the potential uses for the licensed work. For example, if licensing a photograph for use with a journal article, consider also asking for permission to publish the photograph on the journal's web site in connection with the article, or to also publish the photograph in any future reprints, anthologies, collections, and databases that also feature the article.

The chances of receiving royalty-free permission to reproduce a work will be increased if you are able to provide and explain a non-profit, educational, or public interest purpose in, or a public relations benefit from, the proposed use of the work.

> ## CRY ME A RIVER
>
> Writer-actress-director Greta Gerwig's film *Lady Bird* was released to much acclaim in early November of 2017. The coming-of-age drama was set in the early '00s, and as such, it was hoped that the film's soundtrack could incorporate some of those sweet songs that were played incessantly on the radio back in the day. Mindful of the importance of certain music to the backdrop she hoped to set, Greta wrote directly and passionately to several artists, including Justin Timberlake, Dave Matthews, and Alanis Morissette. In each of these letters, Greta rhapsodized about the impact of specific pieces by the artist on her life experience growing up, extolled the deep significance of the requested song to her story and plead earnestly for permission to use it.
>
> Two of those letters were written in August of 2016, more than a year before the scheduled Nov. 3, 2017 release date for the movie. But the third letter was not written until August of 2017 and it appears to have been her first approach to Justin Timberlake. The Timberlake song at issue was by this late date probably already synched into the movie. In her letter, she tells Timberlake that she would love to put his song in her movie because it is perfect to carry the mood of the

> scene. However, she's allowed only three months to pull this off. Moreover, Timberlake does not appear to control the rights to either the musical composition or the sound recording, and she needs rights to both. Presumably, Timberlake has a lot of sway with the music publisher and the record label who do appear to control the rights, but 90 days is not a lot of time to make all these connections. Evidently, it all worked out, as it often does. But had it not, the song at issue was perfectly titled for the moment—Cry Me a River.

RECORD KEEPING

Permission requests should be in writing and should be directed to the Permissions Editor, if a publisher holds the copyright. What we think of as a "grant of permission" is essentially a non-exclusive license. And as a matter of law, non-exclusive licenses do not have to be in writing to be legally enforceable. Of course, if they are not in writing you will always have the challenge of proving that there was in fact a license and just what the scope and duration of that license was agreed to be. So the best practice is to get it in writing. But if that is not feasible for some reason, second best is to confirm in writing (by letter or email) the terms as you understand them, asking for clarification of any term you may have misunderstood or misstated, and indicating that you will act in reliance on your understanding unless corrected.

You can expect the process to take anywhere from a few weeks to as long as six months. You may need to follow-up on the original written request by phone, email, or fax. Also, keep a log of the attempts to gain permission (see sample in templates section at the end of this book). If you receive no response from the rights holder, you may choose to accept the business risk of reproducing material without permission. In that case, a log of the attempts to contact the copyright holder will show a good faith effort to obtain permission.

MINORS

Only a person of legal age can legally bind himself/herself to an enforceable contract. The legal age of majority is set state by state. In most states it is set at 18 years of age. In two states, Alabama and Nebraska, it is currently 19. In Mississippi it is presently 21 for some purposes. If there is any chance that the person from whom you must get permission or consent is a minor, then you must also get a signature and consent from that person's parent or legal guardian. In such a case, you might add language like this at the end of your request form:

I represent that I am at least 18 years of age (or at least the age of majority in the state where I reside if other than 18), or if not, that I have secured the signature of my parent or legal guardian.

_____
Signature   *Date*

_____
Print Name

I represent and warrant that I am the parent or legal guardian of the person signed above and that I ratify his/her assent to this agreement.

_____
Signature of Parent/Legal Guardian

ABIDING BY CONTRACT TERMS

When permission is obtained, it is necessary that you not only understand all of the terms of the permission grant, but also that you abide by all of those terms.

Rights owners may place any number of different conditions or restrictions on a grant of permission. A grant may be restricted as to the geographic territories where the work may be used (U.S. rights vs. worldwide rights), to the particular media in which the work can be used (print vs. electronic, book vs. website, journal vs. database), or the number of times a work may be used. A permission grant may allow the publisher to modify or adapt the work, may restrict the publisher to reproducing only a certain portion of the work, or may require that it be reproduced unaltered. Some rights owners may insist on a review of the final product prior to publication as a condition of the grant, and others may include special terms that can affect the license rate depending on the number of copies published or what other works are licensed for inclusion in the same piece. (See Chapter 9 for a more detailed explanation of the special restrictions often placed on use of third-party photographs.)

It is critical to understand the terms of the grant when a contract is entered into so that you can be certain that you have acquired rights, for an acceptable price, that meet your needs. It is critical to understand the terms when using the work to ensure that you do not exceed the bounds of the grant and thereby infringe those rights the owner did not license to you. Collections of clip art often come with restricted re-use rights. Even Creative Commons works come with some conditions attached.

If permission is granted, you will probably be required to include notice of the grant in the use of the work. Usually the grantor will specify how to give notice that permission has been granted.

PRACTICAL POINTERS AND GUIDELINES

1) When you elect to seek permission, initiate the permission process as soon as possible in the production schedule.
2) Consider all potential uses when drafting permission requests.
3) Where possible, obtain permission in writing signed by the grantor, rather than relying solely on an informal, oral authorization.
4) Carefully review any terms provided by the grantor. Make certain that you follow, and do not overstep, the bounds of any grant.
5) Consider obtaining legal review of any permission contracts or other contracts and agreements related to the clearance of works.

PERMISSIONS THE OTHER WAY

While we are on the subject of permissions, let's look at your policy for granting permission for the use of portions of your work. There are two reasons to do this: first, looking at the issue from the grantor's perspective may help you anticipate, understand, and adapt to the response you are likely to get to your requests; and second, it may lead you to a more enlightened approach to handling requests for re-use of your work.

An admittedly unscientific survey of the published permissions policies of a couple of dozen independent publishers revealed that many of them start out by setting forth a more or less arbitrary benchmark for use of their published works that, in their view, qualifies as a fair use and thus does not require permission or a fee. Some set the mark at 500 words or less, some 400, some 300, some 250, and so on down the scale. Another set the mark at one entire chapter, regardless of how many words. In my view, they're all misguided.

First, US copyright law does not establish a bright-line test for what does or does not qualify as a fair use. Each case is decided on its own unique facts, taking into consideration the four factors set forth in Section 107 of the copyright statute:

(1) the purpose and character of the use, including whether such use is of a commercial nature or is for nonprofit educational purposes;
(2) the nature of the copyrighted work;
(3) the amount and substantiality of the portion used in relation to the copyrighted work as a whole; and
(4) the effect of the use upon the potential market for or value of the copyrighted work. (For more about fair use, see Chapter 2).

Second, to focus any attention on how much of your publishing assets the public may take without asking, especially when the answer isn't clear from settled law, seems like a waste of the attentions of an interested patron and an ineffective way to maximize the value of those assets.

GOOD REASONS TO IMPROVE YOUR PERMISSIONS PROGRAM

Instead of treating permissions requests as a burden to be avoided when possible, consider building a robust permissions and licensing program that will not only be good for your bottom line, but that will also strengthen your copyright portfolio. More specifically, a well-conceived permissions and licensing program will:

- Generate another revenue stream with little additional cost—there is no cost of goods sold and little direct cost or overhead associated with an efficient permissions program. Think of it as a way of squeezing additional revenue out of already acquired assets.
- Aid in the promotion of your core product—extracts from your published works reproduced in other

products sold by other publishers can actually serve as teasers and create a pull through demand for full copies of the source material.
- Aid in furthering your scholarly reputation if you are writing academically.
- Create evidence of a market for licenses/permissions—the fourth fair use factor concerns the impact of the accused use on the potential market for your work. It will work to your advantage in overcoming an asserted fair use defense if you have evidence, in the form of a robust permissions program, that you are in the business of selling license and reprint rights and that unconsented uses thus deprive you of the revenue that would otherwise be generated by a license.
- Create evidence of a lawful alternative—again, it will help you in overcoming a fair use defense if you have evidence that you have made available at a reasonable cost an accessible alternative to reliance on fair use. At least one US appellate court has said that the copyright owner's claim of displaced licensing revenue will not carry much weight if the accused has filled a market niche that the copyright owner simply had no interest in occupying (as evidenced by a lack of licensing or permissions activity).
- Create evidence of a market price—for damages calculations. Your claim to have been financially damaged by an infringer who has used a portion of your published work without a license or consent will be speculative unless you can produce evidence of the value of the license displaced. One good way to do this is with reference to a history of licenses actually granted.

PERMISSIONS BEST PRACTICES

First and foremost, promote your permissions services. Have a policy on your web page and make it easy to submit a request online. Include a description in your catalog and include a blank permissions request or request-for-quote form that permission seekers can fill out and fax or email. Include a statement on the copyright page of each of your books directing readers to your website, catalog, or the phone number/email of your permissions person/department.

Grant rights only as they will be exploited, one edition of the work at a time. Insist that the requestor identify the work in which your excerpt will be used by title, by edition, by language, and by form/medium (hard cover, soft cover, mass market, or e-book, etc.).

Ask the requestor to provide the price, the size of the first print run, and the projected life-of-edition sales of the work in which your excerpt will be used. This information will help you establish an appropriate fee for the requested grant. (See section on "How Do You Price the Grant" for ideas on how to set the fee.)

Make your grant of permission in writing on a form developed by you and make it contingent upon compliance with the following conditions:

- The grant of permission should extend only to one edition of the new work and should not extend to use in any other edition, revision, version, or translation.
- The grant of permission should exclude any quotations or illustrations identified in the selection as having been reprinted by permission of a third party.
- The selection should be faithfully reproduced and should not be changed, added to, or deleted from except with your prior approval.
- Each copy of the new work should include a notice

of copyright in the following form printed in proximity to the selection or on a separate acknowledgment page:
Copyright © 20___ by [your publisher's name, or your (or your company's) name if you hold the copyrights]. Reprinted by permission of [your name and contact info].
- The permissions fee should be paid upon publication or within 6 months of the date of this grant of permission, whichever first occurs.
- Upon publication, requestor should provide you with a complimentary copy of the new work (so that you will know when the new work has been published and can check that a proper credit line was included).
- Make the grant expire automatically seven years from the date of publication of the new work, or if it isn't published within two years of the date of your grant, or if (once published) it is allowed to remain out of print for six consecutive months.

HOW DO YOU PRICE THE GRANT?

Each book, and each extract from it, has a unique value...both in the marketplace and in the context in which it is proposed to be used. By definition, your work has been published, so it has already passed muster in your eyes as a publishable work. Moreover, the requestor has sought to reproduce a portion of it rather than write new copy, presumably because of who said it or how well it was said. So there's really no reason to set your fee at less than the $1-2 per word that one would probably have to pay for commissioned, publishable work. And you should take into account how substantial an extract it is—not only quantitatively, but also qualitatively—is it the kernel of Gerald Ford's rationale for pardoning Richard Nixon or is it two paragraphs of a historian's garden variety account of an event, the description of which could be obtained from any one of a dozen sources. Factor in the commercial value and popularity of the book from which it was taken as well as the projected value and success of the work in which its use is proposed and fit all of this into the pattern of other permissions you have priced.

At the end of the day, the value of the rights requested is what a willing seller and a willing buyer can agree to. But the value of a well-designed and executed permissions program will be greater than the revenue it drops to your bottom line; it will also enhance the value and enforceability of your entire copyright portfolio.

17) DEALING WITH THE CEASE & DESIST LETTER

IT COMES IN A FEDEX ENVELOPE; or by US mail, marked certified, return receipt; or by Express Mail in a blue and white cardboard mailer—as much for impact as for evidence of receipt. The return address is clearly that of a law firm, Abel, Cain & Associates, LLP. Maybe it's a letter about your surprise inheritance from some long-forgotten heir. But more likely, it starts out:

> *Dear Ms. Defendant:*
> *This firm and I represent XXX. Our client advises us that it has reason to believe that your company . . .*
> *[and it's all downhill from here].*

WHAT DO YOU DO NEXT??

If your work has been published by a book or journal publisher, then the letter will likely have been directed to them and you will be forwarded a copy to alert you to the claim. What you do next will be determined by the representations, warranties, and associated defense and indemnification obligations in your publishing contract. If you have a publishing/media lawyer, this is the time to reach out to her. Be prepared first to tell your lawyer who the claiming party is and who your publisher is. Your lawyer will need to know this first, before she can hear about the claim or review the letter and advise you, so that she can clear conflicts—meaning she has to check to be sure that neither the claiming party nor the publisher are a client of hers. Of course, if your lawyer is in a solo practice, there is little chance of a conflict, but some firms have hundreds of lawyers and multiple offices and a conflict check at a firm like this can take one or several days to complete.

Only after the conflict check is completed will your lawyer be able to review the demand letter and your publishing contract and advise you accordingly. If you have media perils insurance coverage, this is the time to tell your publisher that.

If your work was self-published, the letter will likely have been addressed directly to you. Here again, this is the time to reach out to your publishing/media lawyer. The demand letter will probably have instructed you to respond by a specified date, anywhere from a few days to a few weeks from the date of the letter. Don't wait until the deadline to contact your lawyer. Do reach out as soon as you reasonably can, by phone or email.

GOING IT ALONE

If you don't already have a lawyer experienced in copyright, trademark, libel, privacy, publicity, and/or advertising claims and you want to take a shot first at resolving the issue without engaging such a lawyer, there are certain steps you should take and you should take them in a certain order.

First, contact your insurance carrier. Put them on notice of the demand, whether or not you think there is anything to it. Sometimes it takes a while for the facts to be fully developed—your first instinct may not be right and you don't want to risk compromising your insurance coverage by failing to timely report the demand. Depending on the nature of the claim, there may be coverage or an obligation to defend under the "advertising injury" provision of your Comprehensive General Liability (CGL) policy—don't be misled by the description, this coverage is much broader than it sounds. Other claims may require a more specialized policy, sometimes called "media perils," sometimes "errors and omissions," sometimes "cyber-risk" or "cyber-liability" and sometimes "professional liability" policies.

Second, if the claim relates to content provided by a co-author or other contributor, notify that person of the claim as well. Your contract with the person who contributed the content complained of should contain a section of representations and warranties coupled with a commitment to indemnify you for any claim resulting from a breach of those promises. Your contract will probably require you to provide that person with notice of any claim as a condition to their indemnification obligation. Even if the contract doesn't expressly require you to do that, you should do it anyway. You will need their assistance in responding to, defending against, or settling the claim and they can't help you if they don't know about it.

Third, you should write a short letter to opposing counsel, acknowledging receipt of his letter and letting him know that you are undertaking a preliminary investigation and evaluation of the allegations and claims asserted in his letter and will respond to him substantively as soon as you have completed your investigation. Comedian Ron White says it about his first arrest: he had the *right* to remain silent…but not the *ability*. Do not follow Ron's lead. The less said in this initial letter or email, the better. Send your letter by courier or by some other means that provides you with a record of its receipt.

THE QUESTION WORTH ASKING

Notwithstanding the admonition to be brief in this first response, there is one subject you might pursue. Ask for additional information about the asserted claims if the information supplied in the demand letter is incomplete. For example, if the allegation is that some content in one of your books or in a journal article infringes the copyrighted work of some other, ask for a copy of the copyright registration certificate for the allegedly copied work and, if that work is not a readily identifiable, published work, ask also to see a copy of the identifying material that was deposited with the Copyright Office along with the original application for registration. A work does not have to have been registered before it is accorded copyright protection, but whether it was timely registered and how and in what form it was registered will have an important impact on the strength of the accuser's claims and the remedies available to them if they are successful. As another example, if the allegation is infringement of another party's trademark or trade dress, ask to see a copy of any trademark registration for the mark alleged to have been infringed. Again, a mark does not have to have been registered in order to have protection as a trademark, but whether it is the subject of a valid and subsisting registration will have an impact on the opposing party's case. If the claim alleges libel and the demand letter does not specifically identify and quote all statements alleged to be libelous, ask the opposing lawyer to provide that information and to specify exactly what about each statement is alleged to be false. In each case, the additional information will assist you in investigating and evaluating the claim and will help to facilitate a speedier resolution.

DON'T RISE TO THE BAIT

No matter how overreaching or rude the tone of the demand, resist the temptation to be anything other than perfectly polite and respectful in your response. If you rise to the bait and respond defiantly or sarcastically, you can bet that your response will be promptly posted on a website or in a blog for all to see…and the digital attention you are likely to attract will probably be unwelcome. A viral public reaction can be every bit as devas-tating as a final judgment on the merits and your insurance policy may not cover the consequences of adverse publicity. (For a vivid example of how wrong this can go, read about what happened to the publisher of *Cooks Source* magazine in Chapter 1).

IGNORE MOST OF THE DEMANDS, MOST OF THE TIME, AT LEAST INITIALLY

The demand letter will probably ask you to do a series of things by a certain specified date: to freeze inventory, suspend sales, or remove content from your website; to provide an accounting of all sales or distribution; to provide a list and contact information for all customers who bought or received a copy of the accused work; to post an apology and a link to the accuser's website; and so on. There is always the exception, where liability is clear and potential damages substantial, where immediate compliance is the best path to resolution. But in most cases, the better course of action is to not comply with or respond to those demands until after you have completed your investigation and, where warranted, secured the advice of competent counsel.

If the demand concerns allegation of libel, the letter may insist upon a retraction in the next issue of your publication. Your First Amendment rights allow you to disregard this demand, but a state law in the applicable jurisdiction may provide some immunity from certain kinds of damages if the retraction statute applies to you, if the demand was made in the proper form, and if the retraction you publish conforms to the statutory requirements, which will likely include the time and manner in which it must be published. It would be wise to not cut this corner and to get competent legal advice before deciding how to proceed in such a circumstance.

BE CAREFUL OUT THERE

If you can make the claim (whatever it might be) go away without the active involvement of your insurance coverage and your lawyer, more power to you. If, notwithstanding your initial efforts, it won't go away early and a substantive response is required, it is probably best to involve a lawyer. Certainly, if a cash settlement is involved, you would be courting disaster to pay for a release without first getting advice of counsel. At this point, should you get to it, it is likely that your insurance coverage will provide some support. Just be careful what you say, be more careful about what you write, and when in doubt, be silent.

Letter 1 Example

CAIN, ABEL & ASSOCIATES, LLP
2200 PNC Center
84 Fifth Avenue
New York, NY 10110

March __, 2018

Via Certified Mail, Return Receipt Requested

Mary Miller, Publisher
Valiant Publishing, LLC
13925 61st Avenue N.
Bloomington, IL 61701

Re: Copyright Infringement of Half Dome Photograph

Dear Ms. Miller:

    This firm and the undersigned represent the Ansel Trust, repository of the intellectual property rights of the late Adam Ansel ("Ansel Trust"), in the enforcement of its intellectual property rights and in particular the enforcement of those rights associated with the photographs of Adam Ansel. In that connection, our client has advised us that in June of 2015 it entered a license agreement with Valiant Publishing for the reproduction of Ansel's copyrighted photograph of Half Dome as a half-page internal illustration in the printed edition only of a book published by Valiant under the title *Fiscal Cliff, From Above and Below*, by John Public.
    As you know from the terms of the license agreement, the photograph at issue is the copyrighted property of the Ansel Estate.
    Our client has informed us that, notwithstanding the limited rights granted under the license agreement, Valiant has used the subject photograph on the cover of its book, on an e-book edition of same, and in advertising for the book on the Valiant website at *www.valiantpublishing.com* and on the Amazon website. Valiant's use of the photograph in this manner is outside the scope of the license agreement and constitutes infringement of our client's copyrights. The remedies for copyright infringement include: i) an order from a U S District Court instructing you to cease your infringing conduct and seizing for destruction all infringing copies and associated reproductive materials; ii) recovery of our client's attorney fees and costs incurred in connection with the enforcement of its rights; iii) recovery of our client's damages together with any profits made by you from the infringing conduct; or, at our client's election, statutory damages of up to $150,000. 17 U.S.C.§§ 502, 503, 504, 505.

Of course, if there is an innocent explanation, we are most interested and anxious to hear it and we ask that you provide it promptly. If not, we hereby demand on behalf of our client that you:

- immediately cease and desist distribution of the infringing book and that you further provide verification in writing within ten days of the date of this letter that such activity has ceased;
- provide us, within fourteen days of the date of this letter, with an accounting for all sales of copies of the subject book, in printed and e-book form;
- provide, within fourteen days of the date of this letter, a written inventory showing the count and location of all copies and associated reproductive materials (digital and print) and set those materials aside for inspection and eventual destruction;
- disclose, within fourteen days of the date of this letter, any other uses, electronic or print, you have made of our client's work (and if there have been none, provide a written certification to that effect);
- provide, within fourteen days of the date of this letter, an accounting of the date the infringing work was first incorporated in your website together with an accounting of any revenues (from advertising or other sources) or other benefits derived from the operation of your website (other than direct book sales) together with an explanation of how those fees or benefits are set or determined;
- provide, within fourteen days of the date of this letter, a list of any known links to the web page on which the infringing book appears; and,
- agree to cooperate in an independent audit of your books and records for the period in question (destruction of relevant evidence is a separately punishable offense).

We ask that you acknowledge receipt of this letter promptly and that you ask your counsel to contact us within ten days of its date so that we may be apprised of your intentions and avoid an unnecessary escalation. If we do not have your prompt cooperation with the foregoing demand, we have been authorized to serve a takedown demand on your firm's internet service provider. (Courtesy copy enclosed.)

Sincerely,
Abel, Cain & Associates, LLP
Samuel Abel
SA/plg

Enclosure

cc: Mr. Don Ansel, Trustee, Ansel Trust

Letter 2 Example

CAIN, ABEL & ASSOCIATES, LLP
2200 PNC Center
84 Fifth Avenue
New York, NY 10110

March __, 2018

Via Email (compliance@skinnycow-inc.com) and Courier

Legal Department
SkinnyCow
1001 Corporate Dr.
Suite 300
Burlington, VT 05401

Re: Copyright Claim; Takedown Demand Pursuant to 17 USC §512(c)(3)

Dear Madam or Sir:

This letter is intended as a notification of infringement and a takedown demand in compliance with the requirements of 17 USC §512(c)(3). This firm represents the Ansel Trust in the enforcement of its intellectual property rights.

It has come to our attention that Valiant Publishing, LLC ("Valiant"), has developed and maintains a web page which can be found at *www.valiantpublishing.com*. As more particularly set forth in the cease and desist demand we have served on Valiant (a copy of which we have enclosed herewith), we have a good faith belief that the Ansel Trust's copyrighted Half Dome photograph has been displayed on the accused web site without its consent or the consent of an authorized agent and is not otherwise permitted by law. See: *http://www.valiantpublishing.com/catalog/fiscal-cliff* (a copy of which is enclosed). Consequently, we believe that it constitutes an infringement of our client's copyrights. Further, we note that Valiant's conduct violates the SkinnyCow acceptable use policy, Sec. 4bi, found at: *http://www.skinnycow.com/legal/legal_aup.bml*

SkinnyCow, Inc., is identified in the Whois database as the DNS host for Valiant and its infringing web page. We declare, under penalty of perjury, that the information set forth herein is accurate and that we are authorized to act on behalf of the owner of exclusive rights in the copyrighted work. Accordingly, we request, on behalf of our client, that you remove or disable access to the accused web page. Any questions you might have regarding the foregoing may be directed to me.

Sincerely,

Abel, Cain & Associates, LLP
Samuel Abel
SA/plg

cc: Mr. Don Ansel, Trustee, Ansel Trust

RESOURCES

COPYRIGHT BASICS

US Copyright Office – www.copyright.gov
Copyright Clearance Center – www.copyright.com
Creative Commons – www.creativecommons.org

FAIR USE

Copyright Office Index of Fair Use Cases –
 www.copyright.gov/fair-use/
Stanford University Fair Use Resource –
 www.fairuse.stanford.edu/about/

DEFAMATION AND PRIVACY

Media Law Resource Center – www.medialaw.org

RIGHT OF PUBLICITY

California Registry of Successor-in-Interest Claims to Right of
 Publicity – www.specialfilings.sos.ca.gov/sii
State-by-State List of States with Post-Mortem Publicity
 Rights – www.americanbar.org/publications/landslide/
 2015-16/januaryfebruary/delebs_and_postmortem_right_
 publicity.html

ENDORSEMENTS AND TESTIMONIALS

Federal Trade Commission Guidelines – www.ftc.gov/tips-
 advice/business-center/guidance/ftcs-endorsement-guides-
 what-people-are-asking

TRADEMARKS

US Trademark Office – www.uspto.gov/trademarks-getting-started/trademark-basics
US Trademark Database – www.uspto.gov/trademarks-application-process/search-trademark-database

TEXT PERMISSIONS AND SEARCH AIDS

Copyright Clearance Center – www.copyright.com
Creative Commons – www.creativecommons.org
The New York Times News Service and Syndicate – www.nytsyn.com
Washington Post News Service and Syndicate – www.washingtonpost.com/syndication
Books in Print – www.booksinprint.com
Periodical Index – www.pio.chadwyck.co.uk/marketing.do
ProQuest – www.proquest.com
Literary Market Place – www.literarymarketplace.com
International Association of Scientific, Technical & Medical Publishers – www.stm-assoc.org
Reprographic Rights Organizations – www.ifrro.org
Gale Literary Index – www.galenet.com

PHOTOGRAPHS/VIDEO

Getty Images – www.gettyimages.com
AP Images – www.apimages.com
PLUS Registry (Picture Licensing Universal System) – www.plusregistry.org
Google Image Search – www.images.google.com
Internet Movie Database (IMDb) – www.imdb.com
Screen Actors Guild (SAG-AFTRA) – www.sagaftra.org
Writers Guild of America (WGA) – www.wga.org

MUSIC

American Society of Composers, Authors, and Publishers (ASCAP) – www.ascap.com/
ASCAP Repertory – www.ascap.com/repertory
Broadcast Media Inc. (BMI) – www.bmi.com
BMI Repertoire – www.bmi.com/search
Society of European Stage Authors and Composers (SESAC) – www.sesac.com
SESAC Repertory – www.sesac.com/Repertory/Terms.aspx
Harry Fox Agency – www.harryfox.com
SoundExchange – www.soundexchange.com
Production and Library Music – www.tunedge.com
AP Music – www.apmusic.com
The Music Bakery – www.musicbakery.com

ART

Art Resource – www.artres.com
Artists Rights Society – www.arsny.com
Visual Artists and Gallery Association - www.vagarights.com
College Art Association Fair Use Best Practices – www.collegeart.org/pdf/fair-use/best-practices-fair-use-visual-arts.pdf
Cartoon Stock – www.cartoonstock.com
King Features Syndicate – www.kingfeatures.com
Universal Uclick – www.universaluclick.com

INSURANCE

Axis Pro – www.axiscapital.com/en-us/insurance/us/professional-lines/axis-pro/multimedia
Hiscox – www.hiscox.com/brokers/media-liability
Independent Brokers – www.trustedchoice.com/business-insurance/liability/media/

TEMPLATES

Download Word versions of these templates at:
TAAonline.net/resources
Password: GRPSET18

REQUEST FOR PERMISSION TO REPRINT TEXT

[Adam Author Letterhead]

[Date]

[Copyright owner's address]

Re: Request for Permission to Reprint

Dear [Name]:

    I am preparing for publication by the American Literature Press a book of collected readings on the subject of Civil War-inspired poetry tentatively entitled *Battles in Iambic Pentameter* and scheduled for publication in 2020. The American Literature Press is a well-regarded academic publisher focusing on its namesake subject and publishing scholarly books written by some of the leading scholars of our time. As an academic publisher of some reputation, they can afford to focus on titles like this one that, although promising an important contribution to the literature, are nonetheless targeted at a relatively small market.

    In researching the subject, I have discovered your insightful article on the subject of [specify] entitled [specify] and published in [specify] and have found it to be uniquely [tell them their work is important and that it will be included with extracts from the work of other notables, etc.]

    May I have permission to include in my book in printed and digital form and in revisions, reprints, internet editions, electronically stored or delivered copies of all or portions thereof and adaptations for video or other media the article described below:

    [List]

    The American Literature Press is not able to provide me with a budget for reprint rights. Accordingly, I ask that you grant this permission without charge [consider offering a comp copy].

    If you do not control these rights in their entirety, would you please supply the name(s) and address(es) of anyone else to whom this request should be directed.

    Unless you otherwise specify, we will use a standard credit line and will indicate that the material is being reproduced with your permission.

Very truly yours,

Adam Author

Permission Granted:

By: _____

Name: _____

Title: _____

Date: _____

REQUEST FOR PERMISSION TO REPRINT TEXT (ALTERNATE FORM)

[Letterhead]

To: [Permissions Editor]

[Address]

[name of publisher] is preparing a [book, periodical or journal article, web site, etc.] tentatively entitled [title] on the subject of [specify] tentatively scheduled for publication on or about [date]. [Describe any educational or public service motivation behind your project, if appropriate, or any ancillary benefit that the addressee may realize by virtue of the exposure your publication will provide.]

In researching the subject, I discovered your work on [specify] and found it to be a uniquely insightful comment/contribution to the literature [flatter them, stroke their ego, tell them their work will be included with that of other notables...you get the idea].

May I have permission to include in my work, in print and eBook form, [and in revisions, reprints, internet editions, electronically stored/delivered copies of all portions thereof, and adaptations for video or other media] the following material (a copy of which is attached hereto):

Author/Editor: _____
Title/Edition/Volume Number: _____
Article/Chapter Title: _____
ISBN/ISSN: _____
Copyright Date: _____
Page/Illustration/Table Number: _____

The budget for my project is very limited and, accordingly, I ask that you grant this permission without charge [consider offering a comp copy].

If you do not control these rights in their entirety, would you please supply the name(s) and address(es) or anyone else to whom this request should be directed.

Unless otherwise indicated, the credit line will include title, author, copyright line as it appears in the book/journal, publisher and an indication that the material is being reproduced with permission.

If you have any questions about this request, please contact the undersigned at (_____).

Thank you,

[Signature]

Permission Granted:
By: _____
Name: _____
Title: _____
Date: _____

[Leslie Author Letterhead]

REQUEST FOR PERMISSION TO REPRINT PHOTOGRAPH

[Date]

[Photo owner's address]

Re: Request for Permission to Reprint Photograph

Dear [Name]:

I am preparing for publication by Jeremiah Publishers in Gatlinburg, Tennessee, a coffee table, photo-illustrated book on the subject of butterflies tentatively entitled *Butterflies of the Great Smokey Mountains National Park* and scheduled for publication in 2020. Jeremiah Publishers is a small press focusing on quality publications on environmental, natural history, and outdoor recreation topics. As a regional publisher, they can afford to focus on titles like this one that, although promising an important contribution to the literature, are nonetheless targeted at a relatively small market.

In researching the subject, I have discovered your excellent photography on the subject of [specify] and have found it to be uniquely [tell them their work is important and that it will be included with the work of other notables, etc.]

May I have permission to include in my work in printed and eBook form and in revisions, reprints, internet editions, electronically stored or delivered copies of all or portions thereof and adaptations for video or other media the photographs listed and described below:

[List]

The book itself will be expensive to design, lay out, and manufacture and, with a relatively small market and modest sales projections, Jeremiah Publishers was not able to provide me with a budget for photographic rights. Accordingly, I ask that you grant this permission without charge [consider offering a comp copy].

If you do not control these rights in their entirety, would you please supply the name(s) and address(es) of anyone else to whom this request should be directed.

Unless you otherwise specify, we will use a standard credit line and will indicate that the material is being reproduced with your permission.

Very truly yours,

Leslie Author

Permission Granted:

By: _____

Name: _____

Title: _____

Date: _____

PHOTO RELEASE, NO FEE

I hereby grant to the Zoological Society of Columbus, and its licensees (the "Columbus Zoo"), the irrevocable, worldwide right to use all or part of its photographs of me and any adaptation thereof (the "Photos") for distribution and performance via any means or medium in connection with the promotion of its business. Further, Columbus Zoo shall have the right to use my name, professional affiliation, biographical information, picture, silhouette, and other reproductions of my likeness in connection with its use of the Photos as authorized herein and in any associated advertising material.

Columbus Zoo may edit my appearance as it deems desirable or appropriate. I hereby waive any right that I may have to inspect or approve the Photos, their use, or any printed matter that may be used with them and release and discharge Columbus Zoo (and its officers, employees, licensee, and any designees) from any and all claims arising in connection with the use of such Photos, including but not limited to any claims for defamation or invasion of privacy.

I understand that I will receive no fee or other payment for this release but agree to this release in consideration for the potential public exposure I may receive. Further, I acknowledge that Columbus Zoo has prepared the Photos and will take future actions in reliance upon this release. Notwithstanding the aforesaid, I also understand that Columbus Zoo reserves the right to use or not use the Photos or exercise any of the rights granted herein.

I am of legal age. In the alternative, this Release has been countersigned by my parent or legal guardian. I have read this release and have signed it, or caused my parent/legal guardian to sign it, intending to be legally bound hereby.

Signature: _____ Date: _____

Printed Name: _____

Address: _____

Parent's/Guardian's Agreement and Guarantee

I represent and warrant that I am the parent or legal guardian of the subject named above, that I am of legal age, and that I have read and fully understand the foregoing release and agree for subject and subject's heirs, successors, and assigns and for subject's legal representatives to be bound by the terms thereof.

Parent or Guardian

Signature: _____ Date: _____

Printed Name: _____

Address: _____

PHOTO RELEASE, FEE

In consideration for the payment to me of $5.00 and other good and valuable consideration, receipt and sufficiency of which are hereby acknowledged, I hereby grant to the Zoological Society of Columbus, and its licensees (the "Columbus Zoo"), the irrevocable, worldwide right to use all or part of its photographs of me and any adaptation thereof (the "Photos") for distribution and performance via any means or medium in connection with the promotion of its business. Further, Columbus Zoo shall have the right to use my name, professional affiliation, biographical information, picture, silhouette, and other reproductions of my likeness in connection with its use of the Photos as authorized herein and in any associated advertising material.

Columbus Zoo may edit my appearance as it deems desirable or appropriate. hereby waive any right that I may have to inspect or approve the Photos, their use, or any printed matter that may be used with them and release and discharge Columbus Zoo (and its officers, employees, licensee, and any designees) from any and all claims arising in connection with the use of such Photos, including but not limited to any claims for defamation or invasion of privacy.

I understand that Columbus Zoo reserves the right to use or not use the Photos or exercise any of the rights granted herein.

I am of legal age. In the alternative, this Release has been countersigned by my parent or legal guardian. I have read this release and have signed it, or caused my parent/legal guardian to sign it, intending to be legally bound hereby.

Signature: _____ Date: _____

Printed Name :_____

Address: _____

Parent's/Guardian's Agreement and Guarantee
I represent and warrant that I am the parent or legal guardian of the subject named above, that I am of legal age, and that I have read and fully understand the foregoing release and agree for subject and subject's heirs, successors, and assigns and for subject's legal representatives to be bound by the terms thereof.

Parent or Guardian
Signature: _____ Date: _____

Printed Name: _____

Address: _____

VIDEO RELEASE, UNCOMPENSATED

I hereby grant to Joe Videographer ("Joe V"), the irrevocable, worldwide right to use all or part of its recording of me and any adaptation thereof (the "Recording") for distribution and performance via any means or medium in connection with [specify the purpose for which you will use the video]. Further, Joe V shall have the right to use my name, professional affiliation, biographical information, picture, silhouette, and other reproductions of my likeness and voice in connection with the Recording and in any advertising material promoting it.

Joe V may edit my appearance as he deems desirable or appropriate. I hereby waive any right that I may have to inspect or approve the Recordings, their use, or any printed or audio matter that may be used with them and release and discharge Joe V (and any licensee and designees) from any and all claims arising in connection with the use of such Recordings, including but not limited to any claims for defamation or invasion of privacy.

I understand that I will receive no fee or other payment for this release but agree to this release in consideration for the potential public exposure I may receive. Further, I acknowledge that Joe V has prepared the Recording and will take future actions in reliance upon this release. That said, I also understand that Joe V reserves the right to use or not use the Recording or exercise any of the rights granted herein.

I am of legal age. In the alternative, this Release has been countersigned by my parent or legal guardian. I have read this release and have signed it, or caused my parent/legal guardian to sign it, intending to be legally bound hereby.

Signature: _____ Date: _____
Printed Name: _____
Address: _____

Parent's/Guardian's Agreement and Guarantee
I represent and warrant that I am the parent or legal guardian of the subject named above, that I am of legal age, and that I have read and fully understand the foregoing release and agree for subject and subject's heirs, successors, and assigns and for subject's legal representatives to be bound by the terms thereof.

Parent or Guardian
Signature: _____ Date: _____
Printed Name: _____
Address: _____

PROFESSIONAL MODEL RELEASE

Date:	
Model Name:	
Model Address:	
Model Email:	
Shoot Date:	
Session Fee (per day of shooting):	

This release ("Release") is entered into as of the date first noted above ("Effective Date") by and between the Model named above and Jane Photographer, with an address for notice purposes of [specify] ("Photographer").

In consideration of Model's engagement as a model, and for other good and valuable consideration herein acknowledged as received, including the Fee set forth above, Model hereby grants the following rights and permissions to Photographer, its representatives, assignees, those for whom Photographer is acting, and those acting with Photographer's authority and permission ("Licensed Parties").

1. **License.** Model hereby grants to the Licensed Parties during the Term the irrevocable, unrestricted right and license to use, re-use, publish, and republish photographic portraits or images of such Model or in which such Model may be included intact or in part, composite or distorted in character or form ("Images"), without restriction as to changes or transformations, in conjunction with such Model's own or a fictitious name, or reproduction thereof in color or otherwise, made through any and all media now or hereafter known for illustration, art, promotion, advertising, trade, or any other purpose whatsoever. Further, Model permits the use of any printed, electronic or other material in conjunction with the Images. Model acknowledges and agrees, notwithstanding this grant, that the Licensed Parties have no obligation to make use of the rights set forth herein.

2. **Representations, Warranties and Indemnity.** Model represents, warrants, agrees and acknowledges that: (i) he/she is at least the age of majority in the relevant jurisdiction, has the right and capacity to enter into this contract, and enters into this Release willingly; and (2) Model's agreement to the terms of this Release does not breach, violate, or interfere with any prior agreements or applicable law, including (without limitation) agreement agreements with modeling or talent agencies or any other person, company, or entity.

Continued on next page

Model agrees to indemnify, defend, and hold harmless the Licensed Parties and each of their respective officers, directors, employees, agents, and representatives, from and against any and all demands, claims, suits, proceedings, orders, judgments, liabilities, obligations, losses, damages, deficiencies, settlements, assessments, costs and expenses (including reasonable attorney's fees, court costs, interest and penalties) arising out of, in connection with, or directly or indirectly caused by (i) Model's breach of the representations and warranties contained in this Release, or (ii) the use by the Licensed Parties of the Images, including any and all claims for libel and invasion of privacy or publicity.

3. **Release.** Model hereby relinquishes any right that Model may have to examine or approve the completed Images, the advertising copy, printed or electronic matter or other material that may be used in conjunction therewith or the use to which it may be applied. Further, Model hereby releases, discharges, and agrees to save harmless the Licensed Parties from any liability arising out of or in connection with the use of the Images as licensed or permitted herein, including without limitation all claims for libel, invasion of privacy, or publicity.

4. **Fees.** Model agrees that full and complete compensation for the Model's services provided pursuant to this Release and the rights granted herein shall consist of the Session Fee set forth above.

5. **Governing Law.** This Release shall be governed by and interpreted in accordance with the laws of the state of New York. Any dispute, controversy or claim arising out of or relating to this Release, or the breach thereof, shall be settled by confidential binding arbitration subject to a protective order against disclosure and administered by the American Arbitration Association under its Commercial Arbitration Rules, however, Photographer may seek an injunction from a court of competent jurisdiction to prevent any breach or violation of this Release by Model. The place of arbitration shall be New York City in the State of New York and New York law shall apply. Only a single arbitrator shall be used. Judgment on the award rendered by the single arbitrator may be entered in any court having jurisdiction thereof. Each of the parties hereby irrevocably submits to the jurisdiction of such binding arbitration for the purpose of any such dispute, controversy or claim.

6. **No Assignment.** Model may not assign this Release, or any of the rights or obligations hereunder, or otherwise transfer such rights or obligations to any third party, without the prior written consent of Photographer. Any attempted or purported assignment or other such

transfer by Model to any third party without such consent having first been obtained shall be void.

7. **Term.** This Release shall date first noted above and shall continue in perpetuity with respect to the Images.

8. **Notice and Payment through Agent.** All sums due the Model under this Release shall be payable to the Model's Agent, and shall be sent, together with all notice, to such Agent at the address indicated above. The delivery of such notices and payments to such Agent shall be a full and valid discharge of Photographer's notice and payment obligations pursuant to this Release.

9. **Entire Agreement.** This Release constitutes the entire agreement and understanding between the parties with respect to the subject matter hereof, and supersedes all prior and contemporaneous negotiations, discussions and understandings of the parties, whether written or oral. Should any provision of this Release be determined to be void, invalid or otherwise unenforceable by any court or tribunal of competent jurisdiction, such determination shall not affect the remaining provisions hereof which will remain in full force and effect. No waiver or modification of any of the provisions of this Release shall be valid unless in writing and signed by both of the parties.

10. **Acknowledgments.** Both parties hereby acknowledge that they have read and understand the terms of this Release. The parties hereby agree to comply with and be bound by such terms of this Release.

11. **Execution.** Both parties hereby agree that execution versions of this Release can be delivered by electronic mail, facsimile transmission or any other electronic means commonly used for business purposes, and that such delivery is deemed made upon receipt of such electronic or facsimile transmission by the other party. All such delivered versions of this Release shall be treated as an original for any purposes.

IN WITNESS WHEREOF, the parties have executed this Release as of the Effective Date: _____

Photographer
By: _____

Name: _____

Title: _____

MODEL
Signature: _____

RELEASE FOR USE OF PHYSICAL LOCATION

Location Release

Series/ Program Title:("Program")

_____

Production Date(s): _____

[Optional: In consideration of a contribution of $_____,] permission is hereby granted to: ("Producer"), having its place of business at: ["Location address", to access the XXX Museum property located at Louisville, Kentucky on the dates indicated above for the purpose of photographing and recording scenes for the Program.

Permission includes the right to bring personnel and equipment onto the property and to remove them after completion of the work; provided, however, that Producer and its personnel shall be accompanied at all times by a XXX Museum escort and shall comply promptly with any request or instruction of said escort. The permission herein granted [shall include/does not include] the right, to photograph the XXX Museum name logos, and marks, as they appear on the premises and on articles located there and to use such images in the Program.

The undersigned hereby gives to Producer, its assigns, agents, licensees, affiliates, clients, principals, and representatives the right and permission to copyright, use, exhibit, display, print, reproduce, televise, broadcast and distribute, for any lawful purpose, in whole or in part, through any means without limitation, any scenes containing the above described premises, all without inspection or further consent or approval by the undersigned of the finished product or of the use to which it may be applied; provided, however, that images of the premises shall not be used in any adult-themed program or in any program that would otherwise expose the XXX Museum to public scorn, contempt, or ridicule or which would be offensive to a person of ordinary sensibilities.

The XXX Museum expressly disclaims any representation that it has or will clear rights to the use of any artifact, painting, photograph, person, or likeness, whether or not located on the premises and Producer understands and agrees that it is responsible for clearing any rights necessary to the use of same in the Program.

Producer hereby agrees to hold the XXX Museum, its directors, officers, employees, and agents, harmless of and free from any and all liability and loss which Producer, and/or its agents, may suffer for any reason, and further agrees to defend and indemnify the XXX Museums from and against any and all third-party claims, liability, and costs which may result from the distribution, broadcast, or performance of the Program.

IN WITNESS WHEREOF, the parties have caused this Agreement to be signed by their authorized representatives on the dates following their respective signatures below.

XXX Museum

By: _____

Name: _____

Title: _____

Date _____

Producer

By: _____

Name: _____

Title: _____

Date: _____

PERSONAL PROPERTY RELEASE

For good and valuable consideration, the receipt and sufficiency of which I hereby acknowledge, I, the person identified in the signature section below, or the owner of the Property described below, whom I am authorized to represent (the "Property"), agree as follows.

I hereby grant to the photographer/videographer identified below ("Artist"), those for whom Artist is acting, and his/her and their direct and indirect successors, assigns and licensees (all the foregoing, collectively, "Licensees and Assigns"), the irrevocable, perpetual and unrestricted worldwide right and permission to create, use, copy, publish, distribute, perform, display, or broadcast pictures, video, audio recordings, printed matter, and motion picture footage depicting the Property ("Works"), including but not limited to Works including images of the Property which are composite or distorted in character or form without restriction, made through any medium, and in any and all media now or hereafter known for illustration, promotion, packaging, art, editorial, advertising, trade, or any other purpose whatsoever.

Artist agrees to exercise care in the handling of the Property and to return it to me at the end of the Shoot in substantially the same condition as it was when delivered to the Artist.

I hereby (i) waive any right that the Owner may have to inspect or approve the Works or the text or other matter that may be used in connection therewith or the use to which it may be applied or payment or other consideration or damages, and (ii) release and discharge Artist and his/her Licensees and Assigns, from any liability by virtue of the exercise of any of the rights granted herein, including without limitation any claims for libel, publicity claims or invasion of privacy, and I agree that the Owner has no rights to additional consideration, accounting or compensation and that the Owner will make no claim for any reason against Artist or any licensees and Assigns.

It is agreed that my and if different, the Owner's, personal information may be used or disclosed only in connection with the (direct or indirect) licensing of Works where necessary (e.g. to defend claims, protect rights or notify trade unions) and may be retained as long as necessary to fulfill this purpose, including by being shared with Licensees and Assigns and transferred to countries with differing data protection and privacy laws where it may be stored, accessed and used.

I represent and warrant that I am of full age, competent to sign this release, and have the right to contract in my own name. I further represent and warrant

C6ntinued on page 174

that I have the authority necessary to grant the rights contained herein and bind all persons claiming an interest in the Property hereto, and if I indicated below that I am a representative of the owner of the Property, I have the power and authority of such owner to enter into and deliver to this Release on behalf of such owner and I hereby indemnify and hold harmless Artist and his/her Licensees and Assigns, from any claims or damages arising out of breach of this representation and warranty.

    I agree that this Property Release shall be governed and construed according to the substantive laws of the State of New York and the applicable federal laws of the U.S. I have read the above authorization, release, and agreement and I am fully familiar with the contents thereof. This release and the rights granted and waivers contained herein shall be binding upon me and my heirs, legal representatives, and assigns.

Artist (print name): _____

Shoot Date(s): _____

Property Information (Describe property covered by release.)

Description: _____

Owner Information

Name (print): _____

Title/Position (if applicable): _____

Address: _____

City: _____ State: _____ Zip: _____

Signature: _____

Phone: _____ Email: _____

PHOTOGRAPHY/VIDEOGRAPHY PERMIT APPLICATION

Great Parks of XXX County
Commercial Photography/Videography Application

Park: _____

Location: _____

Date of use: _____ Start time: _____ End time: _____

Brief Description of Project:_____

_____

_____

Number of crew: _____ Number of talent: _____

Number of vehicles: _____

Name of Shoot: _____

Props: _____

Company Name: _____

Producer/Contact Name: _____

Client Name: _____

Address: _____

Email Address: _____

Work Phone: _____

Cell Number: _____

If making photo permit fee payment by credit card, please fill out the following information.

❏ VISA

❏ MASTERCARD

❏ AMERICAN EXPRESS

❏ DISCOVER

Continued on page 176

Card Number: _____ Exp. Date: _____

Verification Code: _____

Name on Account: _____

Amount Charged: $ _____

To the fullest extent permitted by law, I agree to defend, pay in behalf of, and hold harmless, Great Parks of XXX County and its Board of Park Commissioners, against any and all claims, demands, suits, losses, including all costs connected therewith, for any damage which may be asserted, claimed or recovered against or from Great Parks of XXX County and its Board of Commissioners and employees, by reason of personal injury and death; and property damage, including loss of use thereof, which arises out of the alleged negligence of Great Parks of XXX County and, or in any way connected or associated with this agreement.

Great Parks of XXX County will be named as Additional Insured on the filming party's liability insurance policy and provides proof of insurance of at least one million dollars prior to the event date. It is understood and agreed that the following shall be Additional Insured; Great Parks of XXX County, its Board of Park Commissioners, all employees and volunteers.

My signature below indicates that I am 18 years of age or older and have read the above information concerning the filming at the above identified park location and agree to the conditions stated and attested to the accuracy of the details of my photography permission.

Applicant's Name and Title: _____
(please print)
Applicant's Signature: _____ Date: _____

INTERVIEW RELEASE

I hereby grant to Sarah Writer and her licensees ("Writer"), the irrevocable, worldwide right and license to use and include all or part of the stories, anecdotes, phrases, or other material that I have shared with her (the "Submission"), whether related orally or in writing, in connection with a book-length work she is preparing for publication provisionally entitled "*[specify]*" and any edition thereof (all editions and versions of same collectively referred to as the "Book").

Writer may edit my Submission as she deems desirable or appropriate and she may alter the facts or circumstance of my story as it is incorporated in the Book for the purpose of disguising my identity or the identity of the subjects in my Submission. I hereby waive any right that I may have to inspect or approve the changes she may make to my Submission and understand that she does not guarantee that they will be finally and completely effective to conceal my true identity. Accordingly, I release and discharge Writer and her licensees from any and all claims and demands arising out of or in connection with the use of such Submission, including but not limited to any claims for defamation or invasion of privacy. I warrant that nothing in my Submission will infringe any copyright or trademark right of any third party nor is it defamatory, invasive of any privacy or property right, or otherwise unlawful.

Writer shall have all right, title, and interest in, and any and all results and proceeds from, the uses authorized herein. The rights granted herein are perpetual and include the use of my Submission in any medium (whether now known or hereafter invented) via which all or part of the Book may be distributed, transmitted, displayed, or otherwise shown or rendered accessible.

I understand that I will receive no fee or other payment for the Submission but acknowledge that Writer has undertaken to interview me, has prepared the Book, and will take future actions in reliance upon my consent to the terms set forth herein. That said, I also understand that Writer reserves the right to use or not use my Submission in the Book or exercise any of the rights granted herein.

I hereby warrant that I am of legal age or, in the alternative, that this Release has been countersigned by my parent or legal guardian and further warrant that I

Continued on page 178

have read this release and have signed it, or caused my parent/legal guardian to sign it, intending to be legally bound hereby.

Signature: _____ Date: _____

Printed Name: _____

Address: _____

Parent's/Guardian's Agreement and Guarantee
I represent and warrant that I am the parent or legal guardian of the subject named above, that I am of legal age, and that I have read and fully understand the foregoing release and agree for subject and subject's heirs, successors, and assigns and for subject's legal representatives to be bound by the terms thereof.

Parent or Guardian

Signature: _____ Date: _____

Printed Name: _____

Address: _____

DEPICTION AND COLLABORATION AGREEMENT

This Agreement entered into on October X, 2010 ("Effective Date") by and between:

as author:

[Specify name and notice address] ("Author")

and

as subject:
[Specify name and notice address] ("Subject") for Author's development and writing of a book-length work covering the life, career, and personal triumphs of Subject ("Work").

1. Cooperation.
The Subject and Author agree to cooperate in the development of the Work and to make themselves available at reasonable times and places as may be necessary to complete the Work and secure their publication and other exploitation. However, to clarify the respective responsibilities, the Subject and Author agree to the following obligations:

    a. The Subject. The Subject agrees to provide to Author the exclusive right to and access to all reasonably available notes, journals, videotapes, audio tapes, interviews, newspapers, pictures, and other documents, tapes, or other items reasonably related to either Work or requested by either Author in relation thereto, for the entire term of this Agreement. The Subject agrees to respond promptly (subject to and taking into consideration the other demands on his time) in providing personal interviews or other reasonable requests for access made by either Author in developing and drafting the Work. The Subject represents that all information he provides to either Author, in any form, is truthful.

    b. Author: Author agrees to diligently research and draft the Work, carefully and accurately incorporating, as he/she deems necessary, the information provided by the Subject. The Author contemplates that he/she will complete an initial draft of each manuscript by [specify]. If he/she fails to do so, Author and Subject may by mutual agreement extend the time for completion. In the absence of any such extension, they shall endeavor to fix by negotiation their respective rights in the material theretofore gathered and written, and in the project itself, i.e., whether one or the other of them shall have the right to compete the Work alone or in collaboration with

Continued on page 180

someone else, and on what terms. Their understanding of these matters shall thereupon be embodied in a settlement agreement. If they are unable to agree by [specify a date 60 days from the manuscript completion date above], this Agreement shall become null and void and neither party shall have any further obligation to the other hereunder.

2. Division of Rights and Obligations.

    a. The Author shall have the sole responsibility for developing and structuring the Work; it is, however, understood and agreed that in the course of so doing the Author shall consult regularly and in good faith with the Subject. After completion of the Work, the Subject shall be provided a reasonable opportunity to review and comment on the Work. Notwithstanding the aforesaid, as between the Author and Subject, the Author shall retain exclusive editorial and artistic control; provided, however, that the Author shall remove any statement or reference that the Subject believes in the good faith exercise of his reasonable judgment will unfairly impugn his character or cast him in a negative light.

    b. Attribution on the Work shall be "[specify]."

    c. The Subject agrees to refrain from preparing, or participating in the preparation of any book-length work, and will not share any information or enter contracts, written or oral, with any other individuals or entities for the development of any book-length work relating to his life and the events described above, or any other work which might directly compete with or injure the sales of either of the Work or any derivative thereof.

    d. Author shall retain exclusive authority to market the Work and to negotiate any publishing contracts and any contracts for the exploitation of any rights in any works derivative of the Work in any medium and by any means whether now known or hereafter devised; provided, however, that a copy of each contract shall be provided to the Subject for his review prior to signing and shall be subject to his approval, said approval not to be unreasonably withheld or delayed. It is understood and agreed that the Subject's failure to object in writing within 10 days of his receipt of a proposed contract, with the reasons for his objection sufficiently detailed so as to permit them to be addressed, shall be deemed a waiver of his right to approve same.

    e. The copyrights in the Work shall be obtained in the name of the Author. As between Subject and the Author, the Author shall retain exclusive ownership of all right, title, and interest (including, without limitation, the copyright and all other proprietary rights) in and to the Work. The Subject agrees to execute, promptly upon Author's request, any and all documents

Continued on page 181

reasonably necessary to record, perfect, or exercise said rights.

 f. Nothing contained herein shall be construed to create a partnership or joint venture between the parties. Their relation shall be one of collaboration on a work intended for publication.

3. Payment.

 a. Royalties. All receipts and returns from the publication of the Work and from the disposition of any subsidiary rights therein shall be divided between the parties as follows:

50% to Subject
50% to Author

except that any monies received by either the Author or the Subject for personal appearances and promotions shall be retained by the Author or by the Subject, as the case may be. All agreements for publication and for the sale of subsidiary rights shall provide that each party's share be paid directly to that party.

 b. Expenses. The Author shall bear all expenses incurred by him/her in the development and drafting of the Work and shall not seek reimbursement from the Subject.

4. Rights to Future Work.

 a. Author shall have, perpetually and irrevocably, the unconditional right throughout the world to use, simulate and portray the name, likeness, voice, personality, personal identification and personal experiences, incidents, situations and events which heretofore occurred or hereafter occur (in whole or in part) based upon or taken from the life of Subject or otherwise in and in connection with the commercial exploitation of the Work and any derivatives thereof, including without limitation motion pictures, sound recordings, publications, and any other media of any nature at all, whether now known or hereafter devised. For the avoidance of doubt, it is understood and agreed that the Author shall make no claim to, nor any claim to any proceeds from, the use or commercialization of the Subject's name, likeness, voice, personality, personal identification and personal experiences, incidents, situations and events apart from and not directly connected to the promotion or exploitation of the Work or derivatives thereof.

 b. Without limiting the generality of the foregoing, it is understood and agreed that said right includes books, film, television, radio, sound recording, music publishing, commercial tie-up, merchandising, advertising and publicity rights in all media of every nature whatsoever, whether now known or hereafter devised, provided only that they are derivative of the Work. The Subject reserves no rights to such uses, except to the 50% share of royalties set forth above.

   c. It is further understood and agreed that said rights may be used in any manner and by any means, whether now known or unknown, and either factually or with such portrayal, impersonation, simulation and/or imitation or other modification as Author determines in their sole discretion. Said rights shall be freely assignable by Author.

5. **Release.**

The Subject hereby releases and discharges Author, his/her employees, agents, licensees, successors and assigns from any and all claims, demands or causes of actions that they now may have or hereafter may have for defamation, libel, invasion of privacy or right of publicity, infringement of copyright or violation of any other right arising out of or relating to any utilization of the rights granted to Author under this Agreement or based upon any failure or omission to make use thereof. Notwithstanding the aforesaid, this release shall not extend to any claims based upon an error, omission, or statement in either manuscript that the Subject identified in writing to the Author for correction or deletion.

6. **Terms.**
   a. The Subject agrees to hold in trust and confidence all material and information disclosed to Author in connection with the Work and not to disclose any such material or information to any third person without the prior written consent of Author.

   b. This Agreement may not be assigned in whole or in part by the Subject without the prior written consent of the Author.

   c. This Agreement shall be governed by the laws of the State of Ohio without regard to its conflicts of laws provisions.

7. **Entire Understanding.**

   a. This Agreement is the entire understanding between the Subject and Author, and no oral understandings have been made with regard thereto.

   b. This Agreement may be amended only by written instrument signed by the Subject and Author.

   c. The provisions of this Agreement shall be binding upon the Author and the Subject and their respective heirs, executors, administrators, and successors.

Continued on page 183

8. Notice.

All notices, requests, demands, and other communications required or permitted by this Agreement shall be in writing and shall be deemed to have been duly given if sent by personal delivery, by telecopy, by express courier service, or, if mailed, postage prepaid, first-class, on the third day after mailing, to the addresses provided above or to such other address as a party may specify to the other in writing.

IN WITNESS WHEREOF and in full understanding of the foregoing, Author and Subject have signed this Agreement intending to be legally bound hereby as of the dates following their respective signatures below.

Author: _____ Subject: _____

Date: _____ Date: _____

PERMISSIONS LOG

Permissions Log

Use Information		Source Information		Form and date of request	Follow up attempts	Date permission granted	Form of credit line	Fee	Conditions, limitations, and notes
Selection title	Where used	Owner name, Address and Contact Info	Title of original work and description of selection to be used						

GLOSSARY

Alliteration. A literary device comprised of the occurrence of selecting adjacent or closely connected words that begin with the same letter or sound.

Allusion. A literary device comprised of employing an expression designed to call something to mind without mentioning it explicitly; an indirect or passing reference

Analogy. A literary device whereby the writer compares two things, typically for the purpose of explanation or clarification.

Arbitrary mark. A type of trademark comprised of a word or words that have some known meaning, but that meaning has no connection to the goods or services with which it is used other than as a trademark. Examples include Penguin or Ten Speed Press.

Assonance/consonance. These are literary devices. In assonance, the writer employs two or more words close to one another that repeat the same vowel sound but start with different consonant sounds. In consonance, the writer employs repetitive sounds produced by consonants within a sentence or phrase, often in quick succession, such as in "pitter, patter."

Colloquialism. A literary device in which the writer employs a word or phrase that is not formal or literary, but which is more commonly used in ordinary or familiar conversation, often regionally.

Commercial use. This is a term that has significantly different meanings depending upon the context. When used in connection with publicity rights it means use to advertise or promote a product or service not connected with or endorsed by the person depicted (a for-profit motive is not sufficient to make a use commercial for this purpose). In photography, a commercial use is in contradistinction to an editorial use. When used in connection with video permitting, conversely, it means recording by any technology for an entity for a market audience with the intent of generating income (a for-profit motive would be sufficient to make a use commercial for this purpose).

Commissioned. A work is commissioned when its creation to described specifications has been specially ordered by the commissioning party in contrast to speculative work or work done on speculation where the person creating the work does so without having an order or contract in hand. In connection with photography, commissioned work is the most expensive type of work because it is staged or shot just for the commissioning party and so the photographer's price will have to cover 100% of the value/cost of producing that work.

Consideration. This term has a special meaning in the context of contract law. One of the essential requirements for the creation of a legally enforceable contract is that the promises of each party be supported by a return promise, or consideration, from the other party.

Copyright. A bundle of rights in a work of original expression that belong exclusively to the copyright owner, including the right to make copies, the right to distribute copies, the right to make derivative works, the public display right, the public performance right, and (for sound recordings only) the digital transmission right.

Copyright infringement. The exercise of any one or more of the monopoly rights of the copyright owner by some other without authorization or a legally recognized excuse or exception.

Creative Commons. An open copyright licensing protocol that includes four basic forms of royalty free licenses (and some combinations of them): Attribution, ShareAlike, NonCom-mercial, and NoDerivatives.

Defamation. An umbrella term that encompasses both libel and slander—essentially false allegations that damage a person's reputation.

Depiction release. An agreement obtained from a person who will be identifiably described or incorporated in text, photographs, or video clips intended for public distribution in which the subject waives the right to assert claims that might follow if his/her image were publicized without his/her permission, most notably privacy rights.

Descriptive mark. A type of trademark comprised of a word or words that describe some attribute of the goods or services with which the mark is used. An example would be American Airlines.

Digital transmission license. A copyright license that pertains only to sound recordings and that permits those sound recordings to be digitally transmitted to the public. It is an analog to the public performance license that concerns the musical composition (as distinct from the sound recording).

Disclaimer. A statement that denies something, most commonly intent or responsibility. The use of a disclaimer is not always effective to accomplish its legal objective.

Disclosure. The opposite of a disclaimer, a disclosure is a conspicuous statement of a fact, circumstance, or relationship that would be relevant to the reader or listener in evaluating what has been presented, or to the prospective purchaser of a good or service in making the purchase decision.

Editorial use. In connection with photography or publicity rights, a use wherein the person depicted is the subject of the story, photo, or recording, and whose persona is not being used to advertise or promote a product or service not associated with or endorsed by the subject. It is used in contradistinction to commercial use and a for-profit motive will not disqualify a use from characterization as an editorial as opposed to commercial.

Euphemism. A literary device wherein the writer substitues a mild or indirect word or expression for one considered to be too harsh or blunt when referring to something unpleasant or embarrassing.

Faction. A hybrid of non-fiction and fiction wherein the historical or geographic setting are factual and some of the characters and events may also be factual but where other details of the story, characters, and dialogue are invented. Faction can create the potential for libel if the writer is not careful.

Fair Use Doctrine. A statutorily recognized exception to the monopoly rights of a copyright owner. See Chapter 2 for a complete explanation of the doctrine and how it is employed.

False light. One of four types of invasion of privacy claim, wherein the writer negligently or purposefully distorts true facts to sensationalize a story or juxtaposes a photograph with unrelated text in a way that invites the viewer or reader to conclude that a person identifiably depicted is associated with something that would be highly offensive to a reasonable person.

Fanciful mark. A made-up word or symbol with no ordinary English language meaning other than as a trademark. An example would be Anova Books, a British publisher of illustrated books.

Flashback. A literary device in the otherwise chronological narrative of a motion picture, novel, etc., by which the writer inserts an event or scene taking place before the present time into the chronological structure of the work

Foreshadowing. A literary device to tease readers about plot turns that will occur later in the story.

Hyperbole. A literary device embodying highly exaggerated claims or statements not intended to be taken as literally true.

Imagery. A literary device wherein the writer employs visually descriptive or figurative language.

Libel. Defamation in written or other recorded form.

Libel tourism. Traveling to a jurisdiction with libel laws favorable to the plaintiff for purposes of filing a legal action in that jurisdiction.

Location release. An agreement wherein the owner or tenant of real property or a residence or facility releases any potential trespass or privacy claims in connection with the use of that property for filming or photography.

Master recording license. A copyright license that permits the reproduction, distribution, and synchronization of a sound recording.

Mechanical license. A copyright license that permits the recording of a performance of a musical composition and then reproduction and distribution in physical form of copies of that recorded performance.

Metaphor. A literary device in which the writer applies a word or phrase to an object or action to which it is not literally applicable, as in "You ain't nothin' but a houndog, cryin' all the time."

Open Access. Used in reference to scholarly or journal publishing, Open Access is the free, immediate, online availability of research articles coupled with the rights to use these articles fully in the digital environment. In the Open Access publishing model, the expense of publication is borne by the author or sponsor rather than the reader/subscriber.

Open Educational Resources (OER). Freely accessible, openly licensed text, media, and other digital assets that are useful for teaching, learning, and assessing as well as for research purposes. There are a variety of OER licensing forms and no single, universally recognized model.

Orphan works. Copyrightable works that are theoretically still in their term of copyright but for whom the copyright owners are not identifiable or findable.

Out-of-print. When a publisher ceases to make copies of a published work available for public sale or distribution, it is said to be out-of-print. In the age of eBooks and print-on-demand, a work is not often truly out-of-print.

Oxymoron. A literary device in which apparently contradictory terms are used in conjunction; e.g., military intelligence.

Paradox. A literary device wherein the writer imbues a situation, person, or thing with contradictory features or qualities (e.g., For the actors, the goal was real emotion, produced on cue).

Paraphrase. To restate the fundamental meaning of another's writing in one's own words.

Parody license. In the context of music, it is something of a misnomer in that it refers to a license to alter or adapt the musical work of another in a way that would be infringing if not licensed (true parody is protected by the First Amendment guarantee of free speech).

Permit. Authorization from the governmental entity managing a particular park, facility, or location to stage a video or photo shoot at that location.

Plagiarize. To pass off the work of another as one's own. Often confused with copyright infringement, although the two are different in that infringement requires that the subject work be still in its term of protection and plagiarism does not.

Property release. A private agreement to waive any claims that might be asserted for conversion, trespass, or privacy violation based on the use of personal (as opposed to real) property in a photo or video shoot.

Public domain. A work of authorship and/or the underlying ideas are said to be in the public domain if their use is not constrained by any form of intellectual property right, principally but not exclusively copyright, or if, once protected, its term of protection has expired. That a work or idea is in the public domain means that it can be freely used by anyone, but it does not mean that it can be used without attribution of the source (see Plagiarism).

Public performance license. A copyright license to perform a musical composition publicly, meaning before a group larger than a family and its normal circle of acquaintances, whether they hear the performance together or separately, at the same time or at different times.

Publicity license. A license to use the name, likeness, or persona of a person in connection with the promotion of goods or services.

Right of publicity. One of the four forms of privacy right, wherein the subject enjoys a right not to have his/her name, likeness, or persona used to promote goods or services with which the subject is not associated without his/her permission.

Rights managed. Used in reference to photography licenses, Rights Managed images are selectively licensed for a limited exclusive use, by market, by length of time, by geographic territory, by medium, and so on).

Royalty-free. Used in reference to photography licenses, royalty Free doesn't mean free. Instead it is a term used to describe a license that provides for an up front, one-time payment in return for which the licensee get relatively broad, non-exclusive usage rights.

Self-Published Work. A non-traditional manner of publishing in which the role of the traditional publisher in converting a raw manuscript to a published book which is then promoted and sold by the publisher, is supplanted by one or more vendors who provide those services at the expense of the author.

Slander. Defamation that is in oral or otherwise transitory, unrecorded form.

Suggestive mark. A type of trademark comprised of a word or words that call to mind a desired association between the word or symbol and the product or service in the customer's mind. Harlequin is a suggestive mark for romance novels.

Synchronization license. Used in connection with music licensing, a synchronization (or "sync") license authorizes the recording in timed relation to a motion picture or moving images, of the licensee's performance of a musical composition. If, instead of one's own recorded performance, one wishes to use an existing sound recording, a master recording license will also be required.

Synecdoche. A literary device by which the writer uses a part to represent the whole (such as fifty sail for fifty ships), uses the whole to represent a part (such as humanity for a person), uses the species for the genus (such as person for humanity), uses the genus for the species (such as a creature for a person), or uses the name of the material for the thing made (such as boards for stage).

Trademark. Any word, phrase, logo, slogan, sound, color, consistent "look" for a series of products, and the total image, appearance or even shape of a product or product packaging that serves to identify a good or service as having come from a particular source.

INDEX

Page numbers in italic indicate tables.

AAUP Statement on Copyright, 38
Adverse publicity on websites, 13, 152
After-the-fact permissions costs, 113, 134–35
Alliteration, 15
Allocation of responsibility for permissions and, 115, 116
Allusion, 15
Always protectable mark, 74
Amistad case, 30–31, 32
Amount/substantiality of portion used, 23, 24–26
Analogies, 15
Arbitrary mark, 74
Art
  about, 11
  copyright owners research for, 111
  court cases and, 105
  fair use and, 105–6
  monopoly rights and, 105
  permissions culture and costs for, 104, 106
  public domain and, 105

resources, 160
risk management and, 104, 105–6
ASCAP, 100, 111–12
Assonance/consonance, 15
Attributions
　attribution license, 18
　scholarly/academic works and, 14, 20, 27, 28, 36, 37, 106, 108
Authorship credit, 14, 36–38, 81–82, 96, 112
Avoiding need for permissions. *See also* Permissions; Risk management
　about, 29–31
　Amistad case, 30–31, 32
　authorship credit and, 36–38
　breach of implied contract and, 31, 34
　circumstantial cases and, 32–33
　co-authorship credit and, 37–39
　copyright infringement and, 31–32, 113, 135
　guidelines and practical pointers, 34–36
　potential claims and, 31
　scholarly/academic works and, 10–11, 36–39

Bennet, William, 85
Blogs, 26, 65–66, 152
BMI, 100, 111–12
Book title protection
　about, 79–80, 81, 85–86
　First Amendment and, 85
　series titles and, 71, 79, 80, 82–83, 85
　single titles and, 82, 83, 85
Books
　copyright owners research for, 110–11
　literary devices and techniques in, 15, *15*
　permissions resources and, 159

request for permission to reprint text templates, 162, 163
song lyrics in text and, 96–97
trademark protection for, 81–82
Brands, and trademarks, 70, 72, 73, 76, 78, 81, 82, 85
Breach of implied contract, 31, 34
Breach of policy or contract, 20, 94, 150
Breach of representation, 118, 123
Breach of warranties, 118, 123
Bridgman Art Library v. Corel Corp (1998), 105

CAA (College Art Association), 104, 105, 106
Canadian libel law, 47
CC (Creative Commons), 18–19, 141
Cease and desist letters
   about and examples of, 148, 154–57
   adverse publicity on websites and, 152
   co-authorship/contributors and, 150
   Copyright Office registration and, 151
   insurance and, 148–49, 153
   legal counsel and, 148–49, 152, 153
   libel and, 151, 152–53
   media perils insurance and, 149
   retraction statute and, 152–53
   trademark/trade dress and, 151
   written responses and, 150–51, 153
CGL (Comprehensive General Liability), 149–50
Circumstantial cases, 32–33
Claims-made coverage versus occurrence-based insurance policies, 133–34
Clearing marks, 75
Clearing rights or permissions, 12, 113, 115, 116, 134–35. *See also* Copyright owners; Permissions
Co-authorship, 37–39, 123, 150

INDEX **197**

College Art Association (CAA), 104, 105, 106
Colloquialism, 15
Colorful descriptions, 15
Commercial speech, 68–69
Commercial use. *See also* Nonprofit educational use
   fair use and, 23, 24, 25–26
   noncommercial use versus, 20
   photographs mad, 89–90
   publicity rights and, 60, 61
Commissioned for personal use, 89
Commissioned photographs, 89, 90–91
Commissioned works, and photographs, 89, 90–91
Common-law literary right, 119
Comprehensive General Liability (CGL), 149–50
Consonance/assonance, 15
Contract law, 9, 136
Contracts. *See also* Written releases
   about, 11
   allocation of responsibility for permissions and, 115, 116
   breach of, 20, 94, 150
   breach of implied contract, 31, 34
   clearing rights or permissions and, 115, 116
   co-authorship and, 123
   First Amendment and, 120
   indemnification provision and, 123–24
   mark owners and, 72
   media perils insurance and, 124–25
   Open Access and, 20
   photographs and, 94–95
   public domain and, 122
   representations and warranties in, 117–23
   right of privacy and, 120
   risk management and, 117, 118, 120

self-published works and, 19
traditionally published works and, 20
Cooks Source (magazine), 12–13, 152
Coppola, Francis Ford, 104
Copyright infringement, 31–32, 113, 135
Copyright law. *See also* Copyrights and copyright protection; Court cases; Fair use; Permissions; U.S. Copyright Office
  about, 10
  authors/publishers constraints and, 9–10
  CC and, 18–19, 141
  common-law literary right and, 119
  exceptions/expiration and, 16–18, 17
  fair use and, 143
  mistakes by authors/publishers, 12–13
  monopoly rights and, 10, 18, 101, 103, 105
  scholarly/academic works and, 10–11, 20
  self-published works and, 19–20
  trademark protection for books and, 81–82
  traditionally published works and, 20
  university licenses and, 20
Copyright owners. *See also* Permissions
  about, 11
  after-the-fact permissions costs and, 113, 134–35
  art and, 111
  books and, 110–11
  copyright protection and, 14
  court cases and, 109, 113–14
  diligent searches for, 108, 110–12, 113–14
  Google and, 109, 111
  media perils insurance and, 114
  music and, 111–12
  orphan works and, 108–9, 114
  photographs and, 111
  pre-authorization and, 112–13

record keeping when tracking, 110, 112, 113–14
resources and websites, 110–11, 112–13, 114, 159
risk management and, 107, 108
videos and, 111
Copyright Public Records Reading Room, Washington, DC, 110
Copyright rights, and trademarks, 81–82
Copyrights and copyright protection. *See also* Copyright law;
    U.S. Copyright Office
  about and, 13–16, 15
  exceptions under copyright law, 16–17
  music and, 98–99
  resources, 158
Court cases
  art and, 105
  Bridgman Art Library v. Corel Corp (1998), 105
  copyright owners and, 109
  fair use and, 24, 25–26, 30–31, 32
  granting permissions/licensing policy and, 144
  Harper & Row v. Nation Enterprises, 25
  high-resolution copies/digital asset file court case, 88
  libel and, 40, 41–45, 135
  Maxtone-Graham v. Burtchaell, 25–26
  music and, 97, 98–99
  Salinger v. Random House, 25
  slander, 41
  Wojnarowicz v. American Family Association, 87
Creative Commons (CC), 18–19, 141
Crichton, Michael, 49–50
"Cry Me a River" (song), 138–39

Defamation
  about, 9, 10
  contracts and, 120
  disclaimers and, 49, 50

fiction/faction and, 48–51
First Amendment and, 40, 43, 45, 47
guidelines and practical pointers, 52–54
libel court cases and, 40, 41–45, 135
libel tourism and, 45–47
media companies court trials and, 40–41
media perils insurance and, 41, 52
resources, 158
retractions and, 51
riht-to-be-forgotten risks and, 47–48
risk management and, 41, 44
slander court cases and, 41
Depictions, 127–28, 179–83
Descriptive mark, 74
Digital transmission license, 102
Diligent searches, and copyright owners, 108, 110–12, 113–14
Disclaimers
   defamation and, 49, 50
   endorsements and, 65, 67
Disclosures, and endorsements, 65, 67–68
Dummies series, 83

Editorial use, 89, 91
Editorial use, of photographs, 89–90, 91
Endorsements and testimonials
   about, 64–65
   blogs and, 65–66
   commercial speech and, 68–69
   disclaimers and, 65, 67
   disclosures and, 65, 67–68
   expert endorsements, 65
   FTC and, 64, 65, 66, 67, 68–69
   Mirror Image Doctrine and, 68–69

reader endorsements, 65
resources, 158
reviewers and, 67
English libel law, 46
Euphemisms, 15
Exaggeration, 15
Expert endorsements, 65
Expiration of copyrights, 16, 17, 17

Faction, 48–51
Fair use. *See also* Copyright law; First Amendment
about, 23
amount/substantiality of portion used, 23, 24–26
art and, 105–6
commercial use and, 23, 24, 25–26
copyright law and, 143
Copyright Office fair use cases index, 26
court cases and, 24, 25–26, 30–31, 32
First Amendment and, 28
granting permissions/licensing policy and, 143, 144
guidelines and practical pointers, 27–28
nature of copyrighted work, 23, 24, 25–26
nonprofit educational use and, 23, 24
parody, 26, 46, 73, 101
photographs and, 87
potential market/value of work, 23, 24–26
resources, 158
scholarly/academic works and, 10–11, 28
Stanford University fair use cases resource, 26
False light liability, 55, 57–58, 128
Fanciful mark, 74
Federal Trade Commission (FTC), 64, 65, 66, 67, 68–69
Federal Trademark Register, 77

Fiction/faction, 48–51
Films (movies), 15, 33, 111, 130, 138–39
First Amendment. *See also* Fair use
   authors/editors' constraints versus, 9–10
   book title protection and, 85
   contract law and, 9
   contracts and, 120
   defamation and, 40, 43, 45, 47
   fair use and, 28
   Mirror Image Doctrine and, 68
Flashbacks, 15
Foreshadowing, 15
FTC (Federal Trade Commission), 64, 65, 66, 67, 68–69

Generic mark, 74, 75
German libel law, 47–48
Gerwig, Greta, 138–39
Glossary, 185–93
"Good Morning to All" (Hill and Hill), 98–99
Google, 109, 111
Granting permissions/licensing policy, 142–44. *See also* Permissions
   about, 142
   best practices for, 145–46
   copyright law and, 143
   grant pricing/value and, 144, 146–47
   reasons for, 143–44
Grosset & Dunlap, 82–83
Gutherie, Woody, 99

"Happy Birthday" (Hill and Hill), 98–99
Hardy Boys series, 82–83
Harper & Row v. Nation Enterprises, 25

High-resolution copies/digital asset file court case, 88
Highly offensive information, 56, 57, 58
Hill, Mildred, 98–99
Hill, Patty, 98–99
Hyperbole, 15

Imagery, 15
Indemnification provision in contracts, 123–24
Insurance
    advertising injury provision in, 131–32
    application process, 132–33
    cease and desist letters and, 148–49, 153
    CGL and, 149–50
    claims-made coverage versus occurrence-based policies, 133–34
    costs, 134
    media perils insurance, 41, 52, 114, 124–25, 132, 149, 150
    policy types, 131–32
    resources, 160
Internet and Internet-based business. *See also* Website/s
    adverse publicity on, 13, 152
    depiction written releases and, 127
    digital transmission license and, 102
    Google, 109, 111
    insurance and, 132
    libel tourism and, 46–47
Interview Release template, 177–78
Intrusion into seclusion, 55, 57, 59

Kotler, Philip, 70

Lady Bird (dir. Gerwig, 2017), 138–39
Lanham Act, 85
Lauber, Manfred, 47–48

Law, copyright. *See* Copyright law
Legal age for permissions, 140
Legal counsel, 56, 136, 148–49, 152, 153
Libel. *See also* Defamation
   Canadian libel law, 47
   cease and desist letters and, 151, 152–53
   court cases and, 40, 41–45, 135
Libel tourism, 45–47
Literary devices and techniques, 15, 15
Location, physical. *See* Physical locations
Logs. *See* Record keeping

Mahfouz, Sheikh Khalid bin, 45–46
Mark owners, 72
Master recording license, 101–2
Maxtone-Graham v. Burtchaell, 25–26
McGraw-Hill, 85
Mechanical license, 99–100
Media companies libel trials, 40–41
Media Law Resource Center (MLRC), 40, 41
Media perils insurance, 41, 52, 114, 124–25, 132, 149
Memorializing searches. *See* Record keeping
Metaphor, 15
Minors and legal age for permissions, 140
Mirror Image Doctrine, 68–69
MIT Faculty Open Access Policy, 20
MLRC (Media Law Resource Center), 40, 41
Models, and Professional Model Release template, 168–70
Monopoly rights, 10, 18, 101, 103, 105
Movies (films), 15, 33, 111, 130, 138–39
Multimedia works, 99–102
Multimedia works and licenses, 99–102
Music
   about, 11, 96

copyright owners research for, 111–12
copyrights/copyright protection and, 98–99
court cases and, 97, 98–99
digital transmission license, 102
guidelines and practical pointers, 102–3
master recording license, 101–2
mechanical license, 99–100
monopoly rights and, 101, 103
multimedia works and, 99–102
parody license, 101
public performance license, 100–101
publicity license, 102
record labels and, 101–2
resources, 160
song lyrics in text and, 96–97
synchronization license, 100
trademarks and, 96

Nancy Drew series, 82–83, 84
Nature of copyrighted work, 23, 24, 25–26
Never protectable mark, 74
New Republic (magazine), 49–50
Newsworthiness standard, 58, 60–61
Nike, 64
NoDerivatives license, 18, 19
NonCommercial license, 18, 19
Noncommercial use, 20. *See also* Commercial use
Nonprofit educational use, 23, 24, 143. *See also* Commercial use
Not of legitimate public concern/interest information, 56

Obama, Barack, 47
Occurrence-based insurance policies versus claims-made coverage, 133–34
Open Access, 10, 20

Open Educational Resources (OER), 19
Orphan works, 108–9, 114
Out-of-print, 24, 109, 146
Owners of copyright. *See* Copyright owners
Oxymoron, 15

The Page Company of Boston, 79
Paradox, 15
Paraphrase, 14
Parody, 26, 46, 73, 101
Parody license, 101
Pathetic fallacy, 15
Penguin books, 82
Permissions. *See also* Avoiding need for permissions; Copyright law; Copyright owners; Granting permissions/licensing policy
  about, 11, 136
  allocation of responsibility for, 115, 116
  art culture and costs for, 104, 106
  clearing rights or permissions and, 12, 115, 116, 134
  contract law and, 136
  guidelines and practical pointers, 142
  legal counsel and, 136
  minors and legal age for, 140
  obtaining and, 137–39
  permissions grant terms and, 141
  record keeping and, 139–40, 144, 184
  requests for, 112, 137–39, 140, 142, 143, 162, 163, 164
  resources, 159
  royalty free license and, 138–39
  written requests for, 139
Permits for public space, 127, 130, 175–76
Personal Property Release template, 173–74
Personification, 15

INDEX   **207**

Photographs. *See also* Videos
   about, 11, 87, 89, 95
   commercial use, 89–90
   commissioned works, 89, 90–91
   contract commitment/accountability and, 94–95
   contracts and, 94–95
   copyright owners research and, 111
   editorial use, 89–90, 91
   fair use and, 87
   high-resolution copies/digital asset file court case, 88
   limitations on use of, 91–94
   permissions grant terms for, 141
   photo release templates, 165, 166
   Photography/Videography Permit Application template, 175–76
   PLUS and, 93
   Professional Model Release template, 168–70
   Request for Permission to Reprint Photograph template, 164
   resources, 159
   retail use, 89
   Rights Managed licenses, 90–91, 92
   royalty free license and, 90–91, 92
   terms of limitations on use of, 93–94
   written releases and, 126, 127, 165, 166
Physical locations
   Physical Location Release template, 171–72
   private property releases for, 126, 128, 129
   written releases for, 126, 130, 171–72
Picture Licensing Universal System (PLUS), 93
Plagiarize, 14, 122–23
Pocket Books, 82
Pollyanna protection, 79, 80, 86
Potential claims, 31
Potential market/value of work, and fair use, 23, 24–26

Pre-authorization, and copyright owners, 112–13
Privacy rights. *See* Right of privacy
Private information, 56, 58. *See also* Right of privacy
Private property/location releases, 126, 128, 129
Professional Model Release template, 168–70
Property/location releases, private, 126, 128, 129
Public domain
  art and, 105
  contracts and, 122
  copyrights versus, 16–17, 17
  "Good Morning to All" (Hill and Hill), 98
  representations and warranties in contracts and, 119
  the web and, 12
Public performance license, 100–101
Public space, and permits, 127, 130, 175–76
Publicity license, 102
Publicity, right of. *See* Right of publicity
Publishing/media lawyers, 56, 136, 148–49, 152, 153
Puffin Books, 82

Random House, 82
Reader endorsements, 65
Record keeping
  copyright owners searches and, 110, 112, 113–14
  granting permissions/licensing policy and, 144
  permissions and, 139–40, 144, 184
  written responses to cease and desist letters and, 150–51, 153
Record labels and licenses, 101–2
Register of Copyrights, 108
Releases, written. *See* Written releases
Representations and warranties in contracts, 117–23
Resources, 158–60
Retail use of photographs, 89

INDEX **209**

Retraction statute, 152–53
Retractions, 51
Reviewers, and endorsements, 67
Rhetorical questions, 15
Right of privacy
  about, 9, 10
  contracts and, 120
  false light liability and, 55, 57–58
  guidelines and practical pointers, 58–59
  highly offensive information and, 56, 57, 58
  intrusion into seclusion and, 55, 57, 59
  not of legitimate public concern/interest information and, 56
  private information publication and, 56, 58
  state law and, 55, 58
Right of publicity
  about, 9, 60–61
  commercial use and, 60, 61
  guidelines and practical pointers, 62–63
  newsworthiness standard and, 60–61
  resources, 158
  state law and, 61
Right-to-be-forgotten risks, 47–48
Rights Managed licenses, 90–91, 92, 138
Risk management. *See also* Avoiding need for permissions; Insurance
  about, 10, 11
  after-the-fact permissions costs and, 113, 134–35
  art and, 104, 105–6
  clearing rights costs and, 113, 134–35
  contracts and, 117, 118, 120
  copyright owners and, 107, 108
  defamation and, 41, 44
  faction and, 48

records during searches and, 112, 139–40
statute of limitations and, 113, 134, 135
written releases and, 127
Royalty free license, 90–91, 92, 138–39

Salinger v. Random House, 25
Scholarly/academic works
attributions for, 14, 20, 27, 28, 36, 37, 106, 108
avoiding need for permissions and, 10–11, 36–39
copyright law and, 10–11, 20
fair use and, 10–11, 28
Scientific Technical and Medical Publishers, 112–13
Securing the Protection of our Enduring and Established Constitutional Heritage (SPEECH) Act of 2010, 47
Seeger, Pete, 99
Seinfeld (television sitcom), 73
Self-published works, 19–20
Semantic satiation, 15
Senegalese libel law, 46–47
Series titles, and trademarks, 71, 79, 80, 82–83, 85
SESAC, 100, 112
Seventeen (magazine), 49
ShareAlike license, 18–19
Simile, 15
Simon & Schuster, 82, 83, 85
Single titles, and trademarks, 82, 83
Slander, 41. *See also* Defamation; Libel
Social media, and adverse publicity, 13, 152
Social Sciences and Humanities Publishers, 112–13
Song lyrics in text, 96–97
Song Stories for Kindergarten (Hill and Hill), 98–99
SPEECH (Securing the Protection of our Enduring and Established Constitutional Heritage) Act of 2010, 47

Spielberg, Steven, 30–31, 32
Stanford University fair use cases resource, 26
State law
    breach of implied contract, 34
    permissions from minors under, 140
    publicity rights, 61
    retraction statute and, 152–53
    right of privacy and, 55, 58
    written releases and, 126–27
Statute of limitations, 113, 134, 135
Suggestive mark, 74, 75
Symbolism, 15
Synchronization license, 100, 103
Synecdoche, 15

Tautology, 15
Television programs, 15, 33, 45, 73, 98–99
Templates
    Depiction and Collaboration Agreement, 179–83
    Interview Release, 177–78
    Permissions Log, 184
    Personal Property Release, 173–74
    Photo Release, Fee, 166
    Photo Release, No Fee, 165
    Photography/Videography Permit Application, 175–76
    Physical Location Release, 171–72
    Professional Model Release, 168–70
    Request for Permission to Reprint Photograph, 164
    Request for Permission to Reprint Text, 162
    Request for Permission to Reprint Text (Alternate Form), 163
    Video Release, Uncompensated, 167
    website for, 161
Testimonials and endorsements. *See* Endorsements and testimonials

Text permissions and search aids, 159
Thai libel law, 46–47
"This Land is Your Land" (song), 99
Timberlake, Justin, 138–39
Tracking effort records, for copyright owners, 110, 112, 113–14
Trade dress, 71, 151
Trademarks. *See also* Book title protection
  about and types of, 9, 71
  availability of, 75, 76
  books and trademark protection, 81–82
  brands and, 70, 72, 73, 76, 78, 81, 82, 85
  cease and desist letters information and, 151
  clearing marks, 75
  contracts and, 120
  copyright rights and, 81–82
  distinctive, 74, 74–75
  distinguishing books and, 80–81
  Lanham Act and, 85
  limitations of, 72–73
  mark owners and, 72
  music and, 96
  Pollyanna protection and, 79, 80, 86
  proactive use of, 73–78, 80, 84–85
  protectability of, 75–76
  registrability of, 75, 77
  registration of, 77–78, 80, 84–86
  resources, 159
  trade dress, 71, 151
  Trademark Office and, 77, 80, 82, 83
Traditionally published works, 20
Travel, and libel tourism, 45–47
Ty, Inc., 85

U.S. Congress, 47, 108
U.S. Copyright Office
   cease and desist letters information and, 151
   copyright owners research and, 110, 119
   copyrights/copyright protection exceptions and, 16–17
   fair use cases index in, 26
   orphan works and, 108–9
   registration with, 13, 21–22
   trademark protection for books and, 81–82
U.S. Trademark Office, 77, 80, 82, 83
University licenses, 20

Value of work/potential market, and fair use, 23, 24–26
Videos. *See also* Photographs
   copyright owners research and, 111, 159
   Photography/Videography Permit Application template, 175–76
   resources, 159
   Video Release, Uncompensated template, 167
   written releases and, 126, 127, 167
Vintage Books, 82

Warner Chappell (music publisher), 98–99
"We Shall Overcome" (song), 99
Website/s. *See also* Internet and Internet-based business
   adverse publicity on, 13, 152
   blogs, 26, 65–66, 152
   copyright owners resources, 110–11, 112–13, 114, 159
   Stanford University fair use cases resource, 26
   templates as Word documents, 161
Werlé, Wolfgang, 47–48
White, Ron, 150
Wojnarowicz v. American Family Association, 87
Written releases
   about, 126–27

depictions and, 127–28
Interview Release template, 177–78
location releases, 126, 130, 171–72
permits for public space, 127, 130, 175–76
Personal Property Release template, 173–74
photo release templates, 165, 166
photographs and, 126, 127, 165, 166
Physical Location Release template, 171–72
private property/location releases, 126, 128, 129
Professional Model Release template, 168–70
risk management and, 127
Video Release, Uncompensated template, 167
videos and, 126, 127, 167

ACKNOWLEDGEMENTS

This book did not write itself. And I did not write it alone. I would be remiss, if I did not thank my clients for giving me a reason to learn what I've learned about the law, the business, and the strategies for clearing rights and securing permissions. Equally deserving of credit are the opposing counsel who have also taught me a thing or two along the way.

But enough about me. This book would never have come to pass but for the tireless efforts of Kim Pawlak, who made up time when I missed a deadline and who spun my straw into better quality straw (to claim that she was able to spin it all the way up into gold would be to presume that she got better stuff on the front end). Also essential was the unwavering faith of Mike Spinella, who was persuaded to take one more risk on a book project for TAA (well, maybe unwavering overstates the truth, but when he wavers it's for good and prudent reasons). Thanks also to Mike for leading me to the Greta Gerwig story that resulted in the anecdote for Chapter 16 and to Rob Perez for introducing me to semantic satiation (it's not what it sounds like).

And of course, I must thank Barbara for her support and indulgence through the long hours of writing…she's perfect for me.

—Steve Gillen

ABOUT THE AUTHOR

Stephen E. Gillen is a partner at Wood Herron & Evans, a 150-year-old Cincinnati law firm focused on intellectual property, where he focuses his practice on publishing, media, and copyright matters. He worked for nearly 20 years in publishing before entering private practice in the middle 1990's. He also teaches Electronic Media Law at the University of Cincinnati College Conservatory of Music, and is the author of *Guide to Textbook Publishing Contracts* and co-author of *Writing and Developing Your College Textbook: A Comprehensive Guide*. Gillen is a long-time member of the TAA Council and a regular speaker at TAA conferences.

"Wood Herron & Evans is excited to celebrate our sesquicentennial anniversary this year. Established in 1868 in Cincinnati, Ohio, the birthplace of considerable innovation, industry and creativity, our firm has been a steadfast partner to inventors, innovators, and business leaders in Cincinnati and beyond in protecting such creations.

We look forward to a future of offering the same high quality and effective legal services, with the same focus, dedication, and integrity exemplified by our firm's founders, that our name has represented during the last 150 years.

> The future is bright—and while the nature of the practice has changed greatly, we have adapted to these changes in the past and will continue to do so in the future."
> —Truman A. Herron, 1973

OTHER BOOKS BY STEPHEN E. GILLEN

Guide to Textbook Publishing Contracts
Stephen E. Gillen
ISBN: 978-0997500400 | Paperback & eBook | 54 pages | 2016 | Textbook & Academic Authors Association

Writing and Developing Your College Textbook: A Comprehensive Guide
Mary Ellen Lepionka, Stephen E. Gillen, Sean W. Wakely
ISBN: 978-0-9975004-1-7 | Paperback & eBook | 325 pages | 2017 | Textbook & Academic Authors Association

ABOUT THE PUBLISHER

The Textbook & Academic Authors Association (TAA) provides a wide range of professional development resources, events, and networking opportunities for textbook authors and authors of scholarly journal articles and books. TAA's mission is to support textbook and academic authors in the creation of top-quality educational and scholarly works that stimulate the love of learning and foster the pursuit of knowledge. Its members are aspiring, new, and veteran authors and come from a wide range of disciplines. Visit www.TAAonline.net.

Also Available from TAA:
Guide to Textbook Publishing Contracts

Download an 11-page sample for a "Look Inside" at
TAAonline.net/guide-to-textbook-publishing-contracts

See what readers are saying:

" Steve Gillen's *Guide to Textbook Publishing Contracts* is not just reading material, it is an indispensable reference, whether you are a first-time or experienced author.

— Michael Sullivan, award-winning mathematics textbook author

54 pages | 1st edition | ISBN: 9780997500400

I've never recommended a law book to my friends (or anyone, for that matter). However, I strongly advise anyone interested in textbook authorship, whether looking forward to a first contract or having recently signed your umpteenth contract, to read *Guide to Textbook Publishing Contracts*. Then remember where you put it when you are finished because you'll want to go back and use it each time you are offered a new contract or amendment.

— Kevin Patton, award-winning author of *Anatomy & Physiology* (9e)

You have more leverage than you think.

In this step-by-step guide by Stephen Gillen, a Partner at Wood Herron & Evans, you will learn the key provisions of a typical textbook contract and how to determine what's important to you so that you can enter into the contract negotiation process better informed. Get the "typical", "better" and "better still" options you can consider when making decisions about what to negotiate.

BONUS! 20 Questions to Ask Your Editor

Get a list of 20 questions that you can employ to learn more about your publisher's plans for, and expectations of, your work — information that will help you evaluate your leverage and your editor's weaknesses.

To order visit: TAAonline.net/guide-to-textbook-publishing-contracts

Also Available from TAA:
Writing and Developing Your College Textbook
A Comprehensive Guide

Download a 17-page sample for a "Look Inside" at
TAAonline.net/writing-and-developing-your-college-textbook

See what readers are saying:

"This guide is an essential tool for anyone interested in writing textbooks, from beginner to seasoned veteran. It's like having a group of trusted mentors sitting on the edge of my desk."

—Kevin Patton, author of *Anatomy & Physiology*

325 pages | 3rd edition
ISBN: 978-0-9975004-1-7 (paperback)
ISBN: 978-0-9975004-2-4 (ebook)

"TAA and the authors have done a wonderful service to us all—textbook, academic, and even trade authors—with this seminal, blood-and-guts guide to the art, craft, and work of authoring. Even though I signed my first contract in 1987, I read every word of this valuable new book and took pages of notes to guide me forward!

— Robert Christopherson, author of *Geosystems*

Writing and crafting a textbook and attending to authoring tasks is a time-consuming, complex—some would say monumental—project, even harrowing at times. This updated and expanded third edition by Mary Ellen Lepionka, Sean W. Wakely, and Stephen E. Gillen, will empower you to undertake textbook development by guiding you through the nuts and bolts of the development process. It also provides essential background information on the changing higher education publishing industry, as well as how to choose a publisher, write a textbook proposal, negotiate a publishing contract, and establish good author-publisher relations.

You'll also get 22 samples and templates, and in a new feature called "Author to Author," you'll get an inside look at how many of the concepts introduced in the book have been put into practice by successful textbook authors.

To order visit: TAAonline.net/Writing-and-Developing-Your-College-Textbook

www.ingramcontent.com/pod-product-compliance
Lightning Source LLC
Chambersburg PA
CBHW070548010526
44118CB00012B/1263